BIBLICAL PRINCIPLES FOR INTERPRETING GOD'S WORD

D1564069

By Cooper P. Abrams, III
January, 2019

Disclaimer

The author of this work has quoted the writers of many articles and books. This does not mean that the author endorses or recommends the works of others. If the author quotes someone, it does not mean that he agrees with all of the author's tenets, statements, concepts, or words, whether in the work quoted or any other work of the author. There has been no attempt to alter the meaning of the quotes; and therefore, some of the quotes are long in order to give the entire sense of the passage.

All Scripture quotes are from the King James Bible except those verses compared and then the source is identified.

Address All Inquiries to:

Cooper P. Abrams, III
cpabrams3@gmail.com
435 452-181
Web Site: http://bible-truth.org

A companion booklet titled *"Expository Bible Study Course - Lesson and Sermon Preparation"* is available from Dr. Abrams

Published by:
THE OLD PATHS PUBLICATIONS, Inc.
142 Gold Flume Way
Cleveland, Georgia, U.S.A. 30528

Web: www.theoldpathspublications.com
E-mail: TOP@theoldpathspublications.com

1.0

DEDICATION

To Carolyn, my faithful help meet for over a half a century.

TABLE OF CONTENTS

INTRODUCTION
Biblical Principles for Interpreting God's Word

It is apparent from all the contradictory teachings of the many denominations and cults of Christendom, that they all cannot God's word. "For God is not *the author* of confusion, but of peace, as in all churches of the saints." (1 Corinthians 14:3) Confusion as to what God has truly said is the work of Satan. The verse tells us God, He seeks "peace" in all the churches. That peace comes from knowing God true word in its purity without distortion. This book seeks to dispel the confusion caused by a false interpretation as the result of ignorance of the principles God has given us to know without question His word and then apply it in our lives.

For the most part, each claim to use the Bible as the source of their teachings which is confusing to anyone who wants to know God's truth. Knowing God's pure revelation, it's vital for salvation and living God's will for the believer's life.

For example, most biblical churches, teach that salvation is by one's faith through God's grace apart from works. However, some churches emphatically teach that good works and religious rituals such as baptism is necessary for salvation.

9

Both may claim the Bible as the source of their belief. Roman Catholics and most Protestants practice baptism by sprinkling, whereas Baptists baptize by immersion. The Roman Catholic Church teaches it is the only true church, and that Peter was the first pope based on their interpretation of Matthew 16:18. No one else outside Catholicism accepts this interpretation.

Even the "Christian" cults such as the Jehovah's Witnesses use the Bible to deny the deity of Jesus Christ, the existence of Hell, and most carnal doctrines of the Christian faith. The Mormons, another cult, use a false interpretation of verses such as 1 Corinthians 15:29 as the source for their practice of baptisms for the dead. They believe that God was once a mortal man who became a god, is married and a polygamist, and was exalted to become the God of earth. They believe if they are worthy, meaning, faith to their church's teachings, and live the Mormon Gospel, plus do enough good works they too can become gods and have their own world to rule. In simple terms they believe they can earn godhood and have a world of their own to rule. Although they now call themselves Christians, in the not so distant past, they were offended at the name, wherein now they are identifying themselves as Christians. No one else accepts their beliefs or interpretations. Seventh Day Adventists and several other churches have their church services on Saturday, the Jewish "Sabbath Day." They teach this based on their understanding of the Bible's instruction in the Old Testament concerning the Jewish Sabbath. They and others ignore Exodus 31:12-17 that specifically states the observance of the Sabbath was given by God to the Israelites. It was not given to be an observance for Christians in this age. Pentecostal churches, the modern Charismatic, and emergent church movement teach and practice speaking in "tongues" and miracle healings are valid gifts of the Holy Spirit today. All fundamentalists and biblical Christian based on the plain teachings of (1 Corinthians 12-14) strongly reject these false teachings.

There are also others who in the past were sound Bible believing churches, who now rejecting God's word and patterning their churches after such worldly things a so-called Christian rock music, false translations, unbiblical practices. At the heart of these modern trends, that turn man away from God's word is often a false or a contrived interpretation of the Bible.

It is easy to see that the many different sects of "Christendom" use the Bible to prove contradictory teachings. Paul Lee Tan, in his book *Literal Interpretation of the Bible* says, "Apparently the Bible can be made to prove almost anything."[1]

May I add that Tan's statement is only true when correct principles of biblical interpretation are ignored and violated. Considering all the contradictions in the various teachings, all supposedly based on the Bible, one must ask the question, *"Who is right?"* Surely, God is not teaching, for example, that one is saved by earning salvation by good works and also teaching man is saved by God's Grace without works. God says, *"For by grace are ye saved through faith; and that not of yourselves: it is the gift of God: Not of works, lest any man should boast."* (Ephesians 2:8-9) There is nothing ambiguous in the words or structure of the verses. God plainly states works do not save and that salvation by God's grace through faith is a gift. Gifts are not earned.

God cannot contradict Himself nor can He lie. The question is then can God's truth be determined with absolute certainty? Hanging in the balance is the knowledge of God's truth and the eternal destiny of every soul on earth.

Where is the problem in determining what is God's true word?

God says in 1 Corinthians 14:33, He, *"God, is not the author of confusion."* Therefore, the problem is not with God, but with finite men who for various reasons misused His word knowingly or negligently. Clearly, men have taken great latitude in interpreting what the Bible says. It should be obvious that God did not give us His written word to be a source of confusion or contention. God gave us His word in written form, whereby it would be available, studied, and examined so that everyone could know His truth. Further, He wrote it in such a way as to be clear and not be complicated nor misleading. He said in 2 Peter 1:20, *"Knowing this first, that no prophecy of the scripture is of any private interpretation."* The word translated "interpretation" is only found in this one verse in the Bible and means "an explanation." Therefore, private interpretations or private explanations meant that what the prophets wrote did not originate with them, but rather as verse 21 confirms, they wrote God's very words as God intended.

> *"For the prophecy came not in old time by the will of man: but holy men of God spake as they were moved by the Holy Ghost." (2 Peter 1:21)*

This is the first principle of interpreting God's written word. That simply means that no one person, church or group has the exclusive interpretation of God's word. The Scriptures can accurately be understood by all. Any of those who teach or preach are only correct in their interpretation when it is based on sound biblical principles of interpretation. This answers several important questions. First, can we absolutely know what is God's truth? Second, "What teacher or church is right?" The answer is that the ones who are right are the ones who correctly interpret God's word. More will be said about this through the article.

However, the problem is that sinful and fallible men have ignored what the Bible literally says and stated what they "think" it says, gave their opinion, what it means to them, or what fit their agenda. Some have based their interpretation on false information rooted in a lack of scholarship in studying the Bible. Clearly, this is not an acceptable hermeneutic,[2] which refers to the science of interpretation. Scripture is not what we think it says or what it means to us, but rather literally, what God plainly stated. In other words, truth is what God literally said and meant when He communicated His word in a known language to those, whom He chose to record it. God chose the correct words, placing them in the proper grammatical order to convey what He wanted to reveal. Sadly, ignoring this basic truth of how God communicated His revelation to us has caused great confusion and division among those seeking to know the Lord and His truth. The tragedy is that it need not be so! Eternal life and heaven are only for those who accept and believe God's truth, accepting Jesus Christ as their Savior.

All this confusion is not caused by God. It would make no sense for God to give us His written word if we could not clearly and accurately know the truth it teaches. That would mean that God authored confusion, which He absolutely denies. It would also mean that a man could not truly know what is right or wrong concerning God. That is totally not acceptable, as God is perfect and omniscient. He does not make mistakes.

For example: When a person applies for a driver's license, they are given a manual to study. The manual contains the necessary instructions for one to pass successfully a written exam. It clearly states the laws that govern driving a vehicle safely using correct grammar, spelling, and definitions of words. Suppose you ignore what the manual states and on your exam, answer the questions with your opinion or what you think the answer should or would like it to be? Your test would be graded by the examiner, based on the law as stated in the manual, and if you did not give the proper answers from the manual, you would fail the exam and not get a license.

God's word is no different. The Bible was written in the language of men and can be easily understood if we follow the proper rules of language. Nothing is cryptic in the way that God inspired what He wanted to reveal. It is not complicated and in fact written very simply that all men can understand it correctly if they wish to. God states in Romans 10:17,

> *"So then faith cometh by hearing, and hearing by the word of God."*

This statement would mean nothing if we could not understand the written word. The question that begs an answer is how can a man have faith, which comes from hearing the word of God, if he cannot absolutely know what that word is? God made sure that men would be able to read and understand His word in order to be saved and live for Him.

God plainly states,

> *"All scripture is given by inspiration of God, and is profitable for doctrine, for reproof, for correction, for instruction in righteousness: That the man of God may be perfect, thoroughly furnished unto all good works." (2 Tim. 3:16-17)*

If we cannot accurately know what God's word is then how can a man accept that the Bible is ". . . profitable for doctrine, for reproof, for correction, for instruction in righteousness: That the man of God may be perfect, thoroughly furnished unto all good works."

The answer is plain, we can know and those who correctly apply the rules of language and interpretation <u>know</u> they are following the Lord in truth. The Lord Jesus Himself said in John 8:32 *"And ye shall know the truth, and the truth shall make you free."* God's word, properly interpreted, frees us from the lies and distortions of Satan who seeks to distort and confuse the understanding of God's word. A belief in God's word overcomes not only, sin and death, but also false doctrine that enslaves a man and *separates* him from God.

John 1:1 proclaims that the Word is Jesus Christ. "In the beginning was the Word, and the Word was with God, and the Word was God." (John 1:1) Verse 14 of John 1 plainly interprets for us who the Word is. "And the Word was made flesh, and dwelt among us, (and we beheld his glory, the glory as of the only begotten of the Father,) full of grace and truth." (John 1:14)

This passage says plainly that Jesus is the Word. They are one and the same. If you corrupt, misinterpret, misuse, ignore or pervert the Word of God, it is a personal attack on the Lord Jesus. It is calling Him a liar and that the false interpreter is presenting the truth. It is a rejection of the Lord Himself in that degrades Him. This should be a stern warning to those who misuse God's Word. The "Word of God" is Jesus Christ.

Note 1 Chronicles 17:3:

> *"And it came to pass the same night, that the **word of God** came to Nathan, saying," (1 Chronicles 17:3)*

The "word" was a preincarnate appearance of Jesus Christ.

Further, God says in Proverbs 30:4-5:

> *"Who hath ascended up into heaven, or descended? who hath gathered the wind in his fists? who hath bound the waters in a garment? who hath established all the ends of the earth? what is his name, and what is his son's name, if thou canst tell? Every word of God is pure: he is a shield unto them that put their trust in him." (Proverbs 30:4-5)*

Did you note in verse 4 God is using pronouns referring the word as a Person? Who then is the answer to the questions in verse 4? Verse 5 explains..." every word of God" the Lord Jesus.

The Proper Method of Interpretation of God's Word is the Christian Mandate

The great need today, then, in determining what the Bible really teaches, is to determine the correct and biblical method of interpretation. If the Bible is the Word of God and God's revelation to man, then surely God would give us a way to discern accurately what He meant. For God not to give us a way to interpret the Bible is to leave the interpretation of Scripture to human wisdom that is at best faulty. To have the interpretation of scripture rest on man's wisdom is to have "flesh" interpreting that which is spiritual.

The word "interpretation" means to arrive at the original meaning the writer intended when he penned the words. The original meaning the author intended is the interpretation and must be found before you can understand, and make the application of the passage. A faulty interpretation will produce a faulty application and therefore it is vital to interpret correctly the Scriptures. Here lies the problem. As stated earlier, many have for various reasons misinterpreted God's word and caused confusion.

Some out of ignorance teach erroneous doctrines. Others, who claim to teach God's word, are dishonest and use the Bible for their personal gain. (See Titus 1:11) Their purpose is not to teach truth, but rather to manipulate it to deceive and influence men for their sinful purposes which involves money and personal recognition. These false teachers deceive many people, but not those who make the effort to know correctly, what God has said. It is my belief that the leaders of false churches and cults know they are in error, but realize the truth would destroy their churches or groups, and they would lose power, influence, and the money that they receive. False doctrine is very profitable.

Often, we hear the platitude that we must not "major on the minors," which is saying that part of the Word of God is not as important as other truths. It implies we do not need to emphasize all the Scriptures, just the major or important parts. A preacher is to preach not only the Gospel, but the all of the word of God. (Acts 20:27)

This espouses the idea that if a preacher, church, or denomination teaches the semblance of salvation by grace, even though it also has many false teachings, is okay because it teaches the Gospel. This is a false assumption. All of what God has said is inspired is by Him. (2 Timothy 3:16-17). To leave out any part makes it incomplete and mixes God's truth with error it becomes corrupt and not His truth. Would God approve if a person never committed a major sin, but only sins that might be humanly considered a minor or less important sin? In God's eyes, _does He not_ condemn all sin? A believer is to accept and live by all of God's word, not just some parts he thinks is more important than other parts. God is the Judge of what sin is and what is not. Further, all of God's word is rightly fitted together. If we do not major on living all of God's word, then are we not sinning when we ignore the parts, we might consider less important. Once a respected mission board president pressed me to accept a practice that violated the autonomy of the local church. When it was pointed out what the New Testament plainly taught on the matter, he tried to defend this practice saying "God has given us great latitude in this matter." I then asked him to provide the chapter and verse in the Bible that his idea was based on and, of course, he could not. As a church planter, establishing biblical churches, I could not be a part of a mission that had such an unbiblical position on God word and His plan for a local church. I had to separate from that group.

Another false concept purports that we really cannot be sure about what the Scripture teaches, but rather what is in one's heart, how we feel about it, or what do we think it means to us. Scripture has only one interpretation. That is what the verse or passage literally states. The interpretation is not subject to what we might think it means, but what it literally states which is determined by applying sound hermeneutical principles. For example, some would say it is not important whether a church baptizes by immersion or sprinkling as it should be left up to one's heart or preference to decide. In other words, the mode of baptism, though clearly proclaimed in the New Testament by the use of the word meaning to immerse, is not important. The word in the New

Testament is "*baptizo*" and means to immerse in water. It does not mean to sprinkle water on someone's head. We often hear that how a person is baptized, regardless of how it is done. It is only important that they submitted to baptism. This idea concludes the specific details of God's word are not important and the specific use of the word of God is arbitrary. It does not seem to matter to those who have no biblical standard of interpretation that baptism other than by immersion is not scriptural baptism, nor what God instituted to be scriptural baptism. It in fact is disobeying God.

The truth is in the details. First, God inspired the New Testament writing to use the word meaning to immerse. Further, baptism by immersion symbolizes the death, burial and resurrection of Jesus Christ and sprinkling does not. (See Rom. 6:1-6) God says baptism is to be by immersion and if we obey, His word one must be immersed. So why would a man or church disregard what God has said and still claim to believe in Him or be operating with His approval? If they truly believed God, would they not respect, fear Him, and obey what He says. Jesus said *"And why call ye me, Lord, Lord, and do not the things which I say?"* (Luke 6:46) Where in God's word does, He tells us that His instructions are up for arbitration?

Do the details and specific instructions of the Bible really matter to God? The only place to find the answer is to ask God Himself and the only <u>non-subjective</u> place to seek the answer is His written word. Therefore, to resolve the matter and find what God wants we must determine what *"thus saith the Lord",* because God is the only Authority. He is our Creator and it is His word! We should respect Him and obey Him. This makes it paramount that one is able to interpret the Bible and determine its absolute meaning because that is what God said. *<u>It is a cunning trick of the Devil, that has convinced some men that</u>* we cannot know accurately God's truth.

The Grammatical-Historical Method of Interpretation

Again, the problem today is not, that God did not give us a method of interpretation. God gave us a method, but many men and churches have refused to use it, or not been diligent in seeking it! The method that God gave is the literal method, or what is called the Grammatical-Historical Method. The Grammatical-Historical method interprets Scripture by taking into consideration the context of a passage, the grammatical uses of the words, and the historical setting in which they were written. The literal method, therefore, *"lets Scripture interpret Scripture."* It is not a new method in any sense of the word, and is the only method in which the Scriptures interpret the Scriptures which means God is the Interpreter.

Surely, God is best qualified to tell us what He means and the literal method is letting God interpret what He has said. The Bible is the complete word of God to man. Being His complete revelation, it addresses directly or in principle, everything that man encounters in life. Revelation 22:18-19, says man is not to add to or subtract from the Word of God, the Bible. In 2 Timothy, clearly God states He inspired the Bible. The verses *tell us that,* "All scripture is given by inspiration of God, and is profitable for doctrine, for reproof, for correction, for instruction in righteousness: That the man of God may be perfect, throughly furnished unto all good works." *(2 Timothy 3:16-17)* When God "breathed" on the writers of Scripture, He superintended what they wrote, and they literally produced the Word of God, completely, accurately, without error. God explains this saying,

> *"Knowing this first, that no prophecy of the scripture is of any private interpretation. For the prophecy came not in old time by the will of man: but holy men of God spake as they were moved by the Holy Ghost." (2 Peter 1:20-21)*

This is called the doctrine of "verbal plenary inspiration," meaning God *chose* each word for its specific meaning. He verbally (orally), plenary (fully) inspired the recording of His written word. God supernaturally inspired or superintended the writers to use each word because that word conveyed a certain and particular meaning. The words God inspired were given to communicate a specific meaning to those who read it. This means that if we find what is the correct meaning of each word, considering its context, normal and customary usage at the time it was used, we can know the correct interpretation. The interpretation is the meaning God wanted His words to convey.

It is the purpose of the book to show that we can accurately properly and know what is God's word. The confusion in understanding God's word is the result of unlearned and/or unskilled men, and some who are dishonest, mishandling the word of God. This does not mean one has to be a scholar or expert to understand and properly know God's truth, but it means that anyone can learn to apply the simple and proper biblical principles of interpretation and accurately understand what God has said. Anyone can discern what is right and wrong and distinguish false teachings from God's truth. He can positively know if what his church or teacher is presenting is God's word or the word of man. It is certainly not the mystery that so many try to make it out to be. It is therefore the responsibility of every person who claims the name of Christ to know what *"thus saith the Lord"* that he not be misled.

Let us then look at eleven principles of literal interpretation that lets the Scriptures interpret Scripture. When we say let Scripture interpret Scripture, we are saying, let God interpret His Word for us.

CHAPTER ONE

Eleven Principles of the Literal Method of Interpreting Scripture

Follow the Customary Usages of the Language

We have dictionaries that are lists of words with their definitions. A word can have several meanings. However, a word does have a limited meaning. As an example, take the word "mountain." It could be referring to many types of hills of various heights and compositions, but it would NOT be referring to a "tree." The customary and grammatical meaning of the word "mountain" is a geographical mound or hill of some sort. It would be improper to imply that when the writer used the word "mountain," he was referring to a tree or anything else.

Biblical hermeneutics accept the words of scripture literally used in their customary historical, cultural and grammatical meaning. Certainly, a word could be used non-figurative; for example, a person could say "He was a mountain of strength." Nevertheless, if used in this manner would be clearly apparent in the sentence that this was not a literal mountain, but the statement was a metaphor. A metaphor is a common tool of writing that uses the characteristics on one thing to describe the traits in something else. For example: "John was a tower of strength." A tower is a strong, solid, and tall structure. To say John is a tower of strength implies that John is a strong, sound, and responsible person.

The Proper Use of Allegory

Occasionally, Bible interpreters incorrectly give Scripture an allegorical or so-called "spiritual" meaning. Allegory[3] means to interpret a story, poem, or picture in a way to reveal some hidden meaning, typically a moral or political one. Thus, allegory will take the words and ignore their literal meaning, as expressed in its words and sentences, and give it a non-literal meaning or hidden meaning not revealed by the meaning of the actual words.

John Bunyan's "Pilgrim's Progress" is an example of spiritual allegory.[4] The ordinary sinner "Christian" leaves the City of Destruction and travels towards the Celestial City, where God resides, for salvation. He finds "Faithful", a companion who helps him on his way to the City. In many instances, many characters "Hypocrisy", "Apollyon", "Mr. Worldly Wiseman" and "Obstinate and Pliable" try to discourage or stop him from achieving his aim. Finally, he reaches the Celestial

City carried by Hopeful's faith. Paul Lee Tan uses the following example of an allegorical interpretation of Scripture. One interpreter allegorically interpreted the biblical account of the journey of Abraham from Ur to Haran as an imaginary trip of a Stoic philosopher who left his sensual understanding and after a time arrived back at his senses! (See Genesis 12) This allegorical interpretation has absolutely nothing to do with Abraham's journey or what the Bible records. Another example of misusing allegory would be to teach that the two pence given to the innkeeper in the parable of the Good Samaritan, represented Baptism and Lord's Supper.[5]

The only proper time to use allegory in interpreting God's word is when the Scripture itself instructs us to do such as in Galatians 4:24.

> *"Which things are an allegory: for these are the two covenants; the one from the mount Sinai, which gendereth to bondage, which is Agar. For this Agar is mount Sinai in Arabia, and answereth to Jerusalem which now is, and is in bondage with her children. But Jerusalem which is above is free, which is the mother of us all."* *(Galatians 4:24-26)*

Galatians 4:22-26 is a biblical allegory. Paul

uses the account of Abraham's two sons. One son, Ishmael was born of the bondmaid, Agar. The other son, Isaac, was born of Sarah, Abraham wife who was a free woman. Ishmael was not the legitimate heir of Abraham, being born under the law that allowed a master to have a son with his bondservant. Isaac was the legitimate son and heir, being born free and under grace. Using allegory Paul explains why Ishmael was not the heir being the product of the law. He makes the point that believers are like Isaac the "children of the promise." Ishmael being born after the flesh persecuted Isaac who was born after the Spirit. Verse 30 *says*, ". . . Cast out the bondwoman and her son: for the son of the bondwoman shall not be heir with the son of the freewoman." In other words, cast out the law, which does not bring salvation. Believers then are saved by grace, which is free. The illustration is clear and there is no hidden meaning in what Paul stated. His use of allegory is clearly explained.

The interpreter must understand that nowhere in God's word is there some mystical or hidden meaning in Scripture that only some special person or church has privy to. Even in allegory, the meaning is clear. There is a great deal of symbolism in God's word, but it will be clear what is symbolized and that it represents some tangible spiritual truth as exampled in Galatians 4:22-30.

The sacrifices, temple ordinances, feasts, and God working in varying ways with the Nation of Israel certainly were given by God in a way to symbolize the coming of Jesus the Messiah, and his vicarious sacrifice for the sins of the world. The symbolism in the blood sacrifices clearly pointed to the Messiah shedding His blood for the payment of sin. Salvation by grace and not works are seen in that Abel offered a burnt offering to God of a sheep whose blood was shed when it was killed. Cain, his brother, instead offered plants from his farming as an offering which God rejected. (See Gen. 4:1-16) God rejected Cain's offering because it was bloodless and was a sacrifice of the works of his labor. Abel's sacrifice was an innocent lamb, killed and offered to God in thanksgiving in obedience to God's instructions. Figuratively, Cain's offering represented an offering of works for salvation, whereas Abel's was an offering of a living sacrifice which embodied the sacrificial shed blood of Jesus Christ.

The source of the error of doctrine in many "Christian" churches can be traced to rejecting the literal meaning and applying a figurative meaning. For example, in the past men deemed as the "Church Fathers" such as Origen and Augustine, rejected the literal interpretation of the Book of Genesis and most of scripture. Origen wrote concerning Genesis 1-2:

"For who that has understanding will suppose that the first, and second, and third day, and the evening and the morning, existed without a sun, and moon, and stars? And that the first day was, as it were, also without a sky? And who is so foolish as to suppose that God, after the manner of a husbandman, planted a paradise in Eden, towards the east, and placed in it a tree of life, visible and palpable, so that one tasting of the fruit by the bodily teeth obtained life? And again, that one was a partaker of good and evil by masticating what was taken from the tree? And if God is said to walk in the paradise in the evening, and Adam to hide himself under a tree, I do not suppose that anyone doubts that these things figuratively indicate certain mysteries, the history having taken place in appearance, and not literally."[6] (underline added for emphasis)

This philosophy of looking at scripture manifests itself in the Roman Catholic Church in that the "Church" must interpret the scripture for the people as they are not capable of understanding God's word for themselves. Improper hermeneutics are the foundation of every false doctrine, cult, and church. This allows them to put any meaning that suits their purpose on any scripture. Thus, the authority to determine truth with them is not what the scriptures literally record, but what fallible men purport it to mean as it suits them.

One of the amazing and important things about the Bible is that God gave to all men. God did not give any man, group, or "church" exclusive understanding of His word. God proclaimed this when Peter wrote:

> *"Knowing this first, that no prophecy of the scripture is of any private interpretation." (2 Peter 1:20)*

The Bible was written, translated so that any man can understand and apply God's truths.

Accepting what the words in the Bible literally mean is a vital part of this first rule. Unless the passage says otherwise, or is clearly using metaphorical language we must give the Scripture a literal meaning. As to the Book of Genesis, it is a literal account of exactly how God created the earth and universe. It is a well-stated rule, "If the literal sense makes sense, seek no other sense."

Examples of Biblical Statements that are to be Taken Literally

Revelation 20:6 is a good example of statements that should be taken liberally. The passage states that Christ will reign for one thousand years after the seven-year Great Tribulation. This reference to a thousand years is stated five times. (See Rev. 20:2-3, 4-6) The thousand years is called the "Millennium" and the verse "literally" states that the time period is one thousand years. Amillennialists falsely insist that these thousand years are only figurative (allegorical) and does not refer to any specific period of time.

However, the words of Revelation 20 plainly state the period to be one thousand years. "And cast him into the bottomless pit, and shut him up, and set a seal upon him, that he should deceive the nations no more, till the thousand years should be fulfilled: and after that he must be loosed a little season." (Revelation 20:3) The literal interpretation does not support their belief that there will not be a thousand-year reign of Christ on earth or a Millennial Kingdom. This is the false notion that there will not be a fulfillment of God's promises literally to Israel of a future kingdom. This is the position of Reformed and Replacement theology.[7] The thousand-year reign of Christ does not fit their theological eschatology so they spiritualize it. They deny what God has literally stated when He inspired John to pen this statement. The question then is why would God say one thing and mean another? What was God's point in stating five times that this period, following the Second Coming will last a thousand years, if He really meant something else? Consider that after the thousand years, Satan is loosed, deceives the nations, go to battle against Christ and the Millennial saints, and then be cast into the eternal lake of fire. If one cannot accept that the thousand years actually means a thousand years, then how would one apply that thinking to the rest of what these verses clearly reveal?

Here lies the problem. If God did not mean a literal one thousand years, then how would one go about determining its "real" meaning? We are told to let the Bible commentator or scholar tell you, because he possesses the education and spiritual insights that ordinary Christians do not have. The problem with this answer is then, which Bible commentator, church or teacher should you trust to have the correct answer? By what criteria do you test each commentator to see who is correct? Do you see the problem? When you leave the literal method of interpreting Scripture, you have no means to determine what the passage says! It is left up to each person to determine for himself what it means without any standard or system of rules to follow. <u>One can make up any meaning that suits him or teacher that impresses him and his listeners. Clearly, this leads to great confusion and makes it impossible to know what God intend to tell us</u>! This false approach to interpretation is the reason some foolish men follow the cult leaders. It should be understood that this plays nicely into Satan's plans. Would God give us such ambiguous instructions? The answer is obvious.

If the Amillennialists and Reformed Theology would apply 2 Peter 1:20 the matter would be settled. "Knowing this first, that no prophecy of the scripture is of any private interpretation." (2 Peter 1:20) Accepting the literal meaning of the words makes God's statement clear, but trying to spiritualize the words leaves nothing but confusion.

Let's us labor the point. It is obvious from reading Revelation 20, that the thousand years is literal and not figurative. There is nothing in the passage that would indicate that this period of time is figurative. Thus, if we accept literally what the Bible says we are letting the Bible interpret itself. The correct interpretation of the passage is that Christ will literally reign for one thousand years on earth after the seven-year Tribulation! The literal meaning of these words tells us what God said. There is no confusion or misunderstanding.

Following what God has literally said we have a clear timeline from the rapture to eternity future.

The question the "spiritualizers" of the Bible should ask themselves is, why did God say literally that this period of time would be a thousand years? Why would He say that, if He had some other period in mind? Why would God then not just plainly state what He meant? Why would He say one thing and mean something else? Clearly, the truth is that God said what He meant. He said Christ will reign one thousand years because that is what will happen. The implications of a literal interpretation of this Scripture are that the Amillennialists are in serious error and is a false teacher, and this is a false teaching that should be condemned and abandoned.

Another example is changing the normal meaning of a word to fit one's theology. The Reformed movement and Calvinism change the meaning of the word "world" to refer to Christians, because they teach that God did not die for the sins of the whole world as John 3:16 and other passages plainly state. Note what Jesus said in John 3:16-17,

> *"For God so loved the **world**, that he gave his only begotten Son, that whosoever believeth in him should not perish, but have everlasting life. For*

*God sent not his Son into the **world** to condemn the **world**; but that the **world** through him might be saved."* *(John 3:16-17)*

The word "world" is the Greek word "*kosmos*" and can refer to the universe, the earth, in general to all mankind or the unsaved human race. It never refers to believers.

The Calvinists interpret the word "*kosmos*" 1 John 2:2 as referring to Christians because the Calvinist believes that Christ did not die for the sins of all the world, but only for the few selected "elect." The rest of mankind, according to them, God decreed to withhold His grace and thus they are condemned to the Lake of Fire with no hope of salvation. The Calvinists changes the definition of the word "world" to mean in certain contexts those God has saved. They refer to Romans 11:12, 15 and purporting that "*kosmos*" in these verses refers to those who are saved. Yet, they once again misinterpret the "world." Verse 12 states *"Now if the fall of them be the riches of the **world**, and the diminishing of them the riches of the Gentiles; how much more their fulness?"* (Romans 11:12) In the context, Paul is saying that because of the fall of the Jews the "riches" meaning the Gospel went to the whole world to the benefit of the Gentiles. Verse 15 reads "For if the casting away of them be the reconciling of the world, what shall the receiving of them be, but life from the dead?" *(Romans 11:15)* Through Paul, and the other Apostles and those who have followed, the Gospel was to be proclaimed to the entire whole world. Jesus said "And this gospel of the kingdom shall be preached in all the world for a witness unto all nations; and then shall the end come." (Matthew 24:14) Note, that the phrase "witness unto all nations" without question shows the scope of the preaching of the Gospel and precludes any restriction or limitation.

The word used by Jesus is *"oikoumene"* meaning the globe, earth, or the world. Mark 13:10 proclaims "And the gospel must first be published among all nations." Further, Mark records that Jesus said "And he said unto them, Go ye into all the world, (kosmos) and preach the gospel to every creature." *(Mark 16:15) Can* there be any misunderstanding when Jesus said "Verily I say unto you, Wheresoever this gospel shall be preached in the whole world, [holos kosmos) there shall also this, that this woman hath done, be told for a memorial of her." (Matthew 26:13) This is a perfect example of fallible men tampering with God's word and ignoring the literal definitions of words to fit their false theology. They falsely conclude, based on their idea that Jesus did not die for the world, that this word cannot mean the

39

world at large. So, they redefine the word to fit their false manmade theology. The New Testament proclaims that Jesus suffered and died for the sins of the whole world, meaning all men, and has offered His mercy and grace to all. Nowhere does God say that all men are saved by the atonement of Jesus Christ. I repeatedly state Christ paid for their sins and OFFERS them salvation. Sadly, most of the world reject God's sacrifice and offer.

To refute this false idea, allow the scriptures to interpret themselves. Note what 2 Peter 2:1-4 states:

> *"But there were false prophets also among the people, even as there shall be false teachers among you, who privily shall bring in damnable heresies, <u>even denying the Lord that bought them</u>, and bring upon themselves swift destruction. And many shall follow their pernicious ways; by reason of whom the way of truth shall be evil spoken of. (2 Peter 2:1-2)*

Also, note the phrase in verse 1, "*even denying the Lord that brought them.*" Why did Peter include that statement if Jesus did not indeed suffer and die for the sins of the whole world? Jesus Christ suffered and died for the sins of the whole world and He bought them with His shed blood. The Calvinist's redefinition of the words is simply feeble attempts to buttress his unsupportable doctrines.

Sadly, as John 3:19-20 and Romans 1:18-23 explains that most men loved their sin more than their souls and they rejected God's offer of grace. Jesus revealed the truth saying

> *"And this is the condemnation, that light is come into the world, and men loved darkness rather than light, because their deeds were evil. For every one that doeth evil hateth the light, neither cometh to the light, lest his deeds should be reproved." (John 3:19-20)*

Jesus said that those who are condemned did not come to the light lest their deeds be reproved. They are condemned not by a hypothetical decree of God, but because they deliberately reject the Light, and do not come to the Light, which is Jesus Christ, and the Gospel. He did not say, nor ever said that He decreed that He would withhold His grace and not offer them salvation. Man condemns himself and is responsible for his condemnation... NOT GOD. Never, in God's word is a decree such as Calvinism teaches found in

41

God's word!

This is a perfect example of eisegetical interpretation of God's word and is an interpretation, of Scripture, by which the process of interpreting a text or portion of text is done in such a way that the process introduces one's own presuppositions, agendas, or biases into and onto the text. This is commonly referred to as reading a meaning into the text. The interpretation the Calvinist accepts is based on his presuppositions found in unbiblical Reformed theology invented by his followers.

Often the Bible uses Figurative Speech

The art or skill of an interpreter, using the proper rules of interpretation combined with good sense, can easily understand an interpretation. In 2 Peter 3:8 Peter says:

> *"But, beloved, be not ignorant of this one thing, that one day is with the Lord as a thousand years, and a thousand years as one day."*

Here the time period is clearly figurative. Note that the verse says one day is "as" a thousand years. The word "as" is the Greek word "*hos*" and means "as it were, or about" It does not say one day is exactly one thousand years. God in using the adverb "as" lets us know this is figurative language. It would be wrong to take this figurative statement as meaning absolutely that a day in heaven is one thousand years. Peter is revealing that time in heaven is different than on earth. God is not subject to time. He is addressing the fact that God's plan for the world is on course even though men might think differently because God has not performed His prophecy yet. Peter is saying, don't judge God's actions and time table by time on earth. It would also be wrong to use this verse to say that when the word day is used in scripture it always means one thousand years. Note that the proper application of language gives the proper interpretation and the Bible (its wording) is correctly interpreted.

The Simile

In the Bible, when a verse is not to be interpreted literally it is clearly indicated. By examining the passage, we know that Peter in 2 Peter 3:8 used a simile. A simile is a figure of speech in which one thing is liken to another. In addition, the context of this verse presents further evidence that supports this view. Peter is addressing scoffers who rejected the truth that Christ would return to earth. He was telling them that God does not operate on our time schedule. A thousand years to Him would be "like" just one day with us or only a short period of time. The point is that God exists outside of time. We cannot apply or limit God to earthly time.

Many have tried to use this verse to fix the purported long ages of evolution into the Genesis account of Creation. They believe that this verse allows for great latitude in interpreting the word "day" in Genesis 1 and 2. However, if we apply sound rules of interpreting Scripture to the passages in Genesis it too shows that this is an erroneous interpretation.

Let us look at this grammatically.

The word for "day" is the Hebrew word, "*Yom.*" By definition, it can mean:

(1) The period of light (contrasted from the period of darkness).

(2) A twenty-four-hour period.

(3) A generally vague period of "time."

(4) An exact point in time.

(5) A year.

For example: Some want to teach that the "days of creation" were long periods of time, which would support evolution or theistic evolution. They insist the meaning of the word "*Yom*" is "long ages." They point to verses such as Psalm 102:2, which use the word in a general sense. "Hide not thy face from me in the day when I am in trouble...." This could mean the day was one four-hour period or it could mean any length of time of trouble. This would be the correct interpretation. However, to understand what the word means you must look at the word in all the contexts it is used. Look at verses such as Gen. 7:11, 27:45 Ex. 20:10, Lev. 22:27, Num. 7:24, 30, 36, 40, 48, 54, 60, 66, 72, 77-78 Psa. 88:1, 139:12, Eccl. 8:16. These verses illustrate an unfailing principle found in every use of the Hebrew word, "*Yom*."

Whenever "*Yom*" is modified by a number, or whenever "*Yom*" is used in conjunction with the idea of day and night or light and darkness, it ALWAYS refers to a normal twenty-four-hour day.

The use of a number with the word "*Yom*" is conclusive evidence that the "Days of Creation" were twenty-four-hour periods of time. The Bible literally says, ". . . the evening and the morning were the **first** day." The use of the words, evening, morning and first, limits the meaning of the word "day" to a twenty-four-hour period of time. That is the normal use of the word and exactly what it says. To interpret the time period, which is stated here as meaning anything, but a twenty-four-hour period, is a gross grammatical error in interpreting what the God the Writer meant.

Further, evidence is found in Exodus 20:11. The wording of this verse supports the conclusion that the days in Genesis 1, are twenty-four-hour period of time. Note the statement of Moses, "For in six days the Lord made the heavens and the earth, the sea and all that is in them, and rested on the seventh day: therefore the LORD blessed the Sabbath day and made it holy." This is as clear a statement of the period of Creation as can be had. Moses in connecting the six-day Creation with instructions concerning the Sabbath day is conclusive evidence that the Creation was accomplished in six literal twenty-four-hour periods.

Peter, in 2 Peter 3:8, is assuring believers that God will keep his promises to us. It is pointing out that God is not confined to time as we know it. The use of the phrase "a thousand years is as but a day with the Lord" is understood as being a metaphorical reference to the fact God is not limited by time. He is saying what we might perceive as a delay in time is within the structure of God's plan for the world.

If you interpret 2 Peter 3:8, literally, then you would still have only seven thousand years for God to complete the Creation. You would still not have the billions of years the evolutionist insists it took to create the world and life as we know it. In any case, you cannot honestly use this passage as a precedent to interpret the "days" of Genesis 1, as being anything other than a twenty-four-hour period of time. The result of applying this principle of interpretation produces conclusive evidence that the one thousand years referred to in Revelation 20:6 is literally a time period of a thousand years. We then can be dogmatic in stating the Amillennialists and Reformed Theology are wrong in their interpretation and the correct interpretation is there will be a literal one-thousand-year Millennial reign of Jesus Christ. To accept any other interpretation is in reality calling God a liar or misleading us.

The rule is this: "Always accept the literal meaning of the words of the passage unless there is strong evidence to do otherwise." As stated earlier, "If the literal sense makes, sense, seek no other sense."

Available Reference Materials to Help With Our Interpretation

We are very fortunate to live in this age. Excellent Bible helps are available to help us find the original meaning of a word. One does not need to read Greek or Hebrew to understand the meanings of words in the original languages. Available are Bible Hand Books, Concordances, Bible Dictionaries, Word Study Books, Greek Lexicons, Commentaries, and Study Bibles. For a list of these books, with explanations of their contents, please see the Appendix at the end of this book. There is a wealth of information to be found in books on geography, history, culture and a host of other subjects to aid the serious Bible student.

The Use of Metaphorical Language

Metaphorical language is the use of metaphor, which transfers the meaning of one word on to another. The metaphor is like a simile, but does not use the terms "like" or "as" in making its comparison. For example, a simile would be, "The man was strong as (or like) an ox" or "She sang like a bird." The woman's singing is compared to the beautiful song of a bird.

The following are biblical metaphors:

"Keep me as the apple of the eye, hide me under the shadow of thy wings." (Psa. 71:8)

"For the LORD thy God is a consuming fire, even a jealous God." (Deuteronomy 4:24)

"As the hart panteth after the water brooks, so panteth my soul after thee, O God." (Psalms 42:1)

The metaphor gives effect, dimension, or emphasis to a sentence. God is stating, He is a jealous God, whose wrath is as a consuming fire, accentuates the degree of His displeasure.

Metaphorical language is not to be taken literally. For example: Deuteronomy 32:4 states,

"He is the Rock, his work is perfect: for all his ways are judgment: a God of truth and without iniquity, just and right is he."

48

Certainly, God is not literally a rock. Moreover, the statement is referring to God's immutability (unchanging) and His absolute trustworthiness, which are attributes of stone.

The Mormons teach that God (their god) is a physical man of "flesh and bone" the same as any human on earth. They refer to the Scriptures, which refer to the hand of God as proof that God has a physical body. They proudly claim that they are simply interpreting God's word literally. When the Bible or any literature uses, such language to illustrate a point it is using anthropomorphism, which is giving something that is non-human, the physical characteristics of a human or vice versa. Example: Psalm 17:8 says,

"Keep me as the apple of the eye, hide me under the shadow of thy wings."

If we applied the Mormons method of interpretation, one would have to conclude that God is a bird with wings. Clearly, the statements are metaphorical statements that attribute physical characteristics to God a bird protecting its young, and are not to be taken literally. God plainly states there is no other God and that God is Spirit. (See Deut. 4:39, Hosea 11:9, Mal. 3:6, 2 Sam. 7:22, Psa. 86:10, Isa. 45:5, John 4:24, 2 Cor. 3:17, 1 Tim. 1:17)

God says in John 4:24 that He is Spirit. He

says He is not a man nor ever was a man. Therefore, it is incorrect to say that our Creator, who is the real God, is a god of flesh and bone because the Bible uses metaphorical language to describe the actions of God.

The Importance of Syntax in Interpreting Scripture

Important to arriving at the correct meaning of a word is the study of syntax. Syntax is the study of the word in its grammatical setting. It deals with understanding the word's grammatical use as a verb, noun, adjective, adverb or other parts of speech. It also seeks to decide the tense, mood, voice, and the case of a word.

A Declarative Syntax: *"For the LORD thy God is a consuming fire, even a jealous God."* (Deuteronomy 4:24)

An Imperative Syntax: *"For thou shalt worship no other god: for the LORD, whose name is Jealous, is a jealous God:"* (Exodus 34:14)

An Interrogative Syntax: *"O ye sons of men, how long will ye turn my glory into shame? how long will ye love vanity, and seek after leasing? Selah."* (Psalms 4:2)

The meaning of the phrase *"office of a bishop"* in 1 Timothy 3:1 is only one Greek word *"apiskope."* The translation of the phrase is determined by the syntax. The word "*apiskope*" is a verb, not a noun, and therefore syntax with the grammar of the word, tells us the correct interpretation of the phrase is simply "*If a man desires the "ministry of overseership*." If it were a noun, then the word "office" would apply, but being a verb, it limits the desire to one of service and ministry, not to an official office. The correct translation means Paul was addressing the service or ministry of a bishop and not establishing an "official" office or authority. The emphasis makes it clear that if a man desired the work or ministry of a servant to the congregation, he desired a good work. Further, this equally applies in 1 Timothy 3:7 and the syntax of the sentence limits the meaning to stating ". . . The ministry of a servant."

This also applies to 1 Timothy 3:10, "And let these also first be proved; then let them use the office of a deacon, being *found* blameless." (1 Timothy 3:10) New Testament does not teach or establish an official "office" of a "deacon," but rather Paul is addressing the role of a faithful servant in a congregation and absolutely not an official position of authority or office. This proper interpretation clarifies the use of elected men who serve the congregation, but are not rulers with any authority over an assembly.

Following the Customary Use of the Words in the Original Language

When God used a particular word, He did so to convey a particular meaning. You cannot ignore the customary definition and grammatical meaning of a word, in its historical setting and honestly claim to arrive at a proper interpretation of the passage or God's meaning in His statement. To ignore this principle of biblical interpretation is to destroy the very Word of God itself. This is an attack on the Person of Jesus Christ, who is the Word. (John 1:1,14) God did not give us a subjective and confusing method of understanding His Word. God chose each word for its precise meaning, recorded it, and preserved it so there would be no confusion. Any other method of examining Scripture other than the literal method is illogical and unacceptable.

Applying proper hermeneutics will consider the English word's definition and its meaning in the original language of Greek, Hebrew, or Aramaic.

For example: Look at the word translated in our English Bible "church" which is the Greek word "*ekklesia.*" If you were to look up the word in Vines Dictionary of New Testament Words, or any Bible dictionary, it would refer you to the word "assembly or "congregation."[8]

If you look for the definition of the word "church" in an English dictionary you would find at least five definitions:

1 A building for public Christian worship.

2 Public worship of God or a religious service in such a building: To attend church regularly.

3 The whole body of Christian believers; sometimes with the initial capital letter Christendom.

4 Any division of this body professing the same creed and acknowledging the same ecclesiastical authority; a Christian denomination: the Methodist Church.

5 A part of the whole Christian body, or of a particular denomination, belonging to the same city, country, nation, etc.

6 A body of Christians worshipping in a particular building or constituting one congregation: She is a member of this church.

7 An Ecclesiastical organization, power, and affairs, as distinguished from the state: separation of church and state; The missionary went wherever the church sent him.[9]

I once heard a pastor say all he needed to understand the words of the Bible was a good English dictionary. However, many Greek words translated into English do not show the more precise meaning of its original language. For example, the word "church" in English can have at least seven definitions. I wonder which English definition this pastor would choose. The fact is that none of English definitions convey the meaning of the Greek word "*ekklesia*" that is translated "church" in our English Bibles. It is easy to see the problem in just consulting an English dictionary.

The Greek definition of the word "*ekklesia*" means an "assembly." Colon Brown defines "*ekklesia*" as:

"1. (a) *ekklesia*, derived via *ek-kaleo*, which was used for the summons to the army to assemble, from *kaleo*, to call (--. Call). It is attested from Eur. and Hdt. onwards (5th cent. B.C.), and denotes in the usage of antiquity the popular assembly of the competent full citizens of the polis, city."[3]

Vines defines the word as:

"1. ekklesia (1577), from *ek*, "out of," and *klesis,* "a calling" (*kaleo*, "to call"), was used among the Greeks of a body of citizens "gathered" to discuss the affairs of state, Acts 19:39. In the Sept. it is used to designate the "gathering" of Israel, summoned for any definite purpose, or a "gathering" regarded as representative of the whole nation. In Acts 7:38 it is used of Israel; in 19:32, 41, of a riotous mob."[4]

An examination of the Greek word "*ekklesia*" reveals that the word refers to a group of persons that are organized together for a common purpose and who assemble together for a meeting. Acts 19:32, 39, 41 demonstrates this word was used to refer to a civil assembly of local towns people of Ephesus which included idol makers.

> *"Some therefore cried one thing, and some another: for the assembly [ekklesia] was confused; and the more part knew not wherefore they were come together." (Acts 19:32)*[10]

Without being modified, the word *ekklesia* by itself does not reveal who was meeting. To understand whom the noun *ekklesia* was who was meeting, the word must be modified. Example:

> *"And when they were come to Jerusalem, they were received of the church [ekklesia], and of the apostles and elders, and they declared all things that God had done with them." (Acts 15:4)*

The verse states this assembly was believers in Jerusalem, thus the Jerusalem congregation.

Paul always understands *ekklesia* as a living, assembled congregation of believers in a specific geographical location. This is expressed particularly through the New Testament. Example;

> *"I commend unto you Phebe our sister, which is a servant of the church [ekklesia] which is at Cenchrea:"* (Romans 16:1)

Phebe served in the assembly or congregation at Cenchrea.

Thus, the definition of the word "church" which is the word *ekklesia* in the Greek text when modified refers to a group of assembled believers meeting in a specific geographical location. God's using the word that means "an assembly," precludes any other definition or interpretation. The doctrinal application of this means the word cannot refer to a universal, catholic, or worldwide church.[11] Researching the word in Greek dictionaries refutes the false teaching of a universal church made up of all believers everywhere under the head of some hierarchical authority such as the Roman Catholic Church led by a pope. The only time the New Testament refers to all Christians being assembled together is at the rapture. (See 1 Thess. 4:17)

This illustration shows the importance in determining the correct definition of words in arriving at a correct interpretation of God's word. A good Bible dictionary, or lexicon should be consulted to determine correctly the word definitions in scripture.

CHAPTER TWO
Dispensational Truth

COMMIT NO HISTORICAL OR CULTURAL BLUNDERS

The Bible was written over a period of about 1400 years. During that time, many historical and cultural changes have taken place. God over these long periods worked with different peoples in different ways, but was consistent in revealing His word to man. This is expressed in what is termed "dispensational truth" or dispensational theology."[12] Dispensation is a reference to history.

Biblical history is best grasped when it is understood that God worked differently at different times with different people throughout history. Christians today do not have a temple, temple ordinances, sacrifices, feasts, worship on Saturday, follow the Old Testament or Mosaic Law. Christians living in this age are not Old Testament saints or Israel. Believers gathered in churches (ekklesia) today is a totally different entity or institution than those in the Old Testament.

There are seven dispensations or economies in the Bible. In six of the dispensations God was working with a particular entity in past biblical history. The seven dispensations are:

1. <u>The Dispensation of Innocence</u> – Gen. 1:28-3:13. God was working with Adam and Eve in the beginning. Adam and Eve were the innocent of sin before they sinned.

2. <u>The Dispensation of Conscience</u> – Gen. 3:22-7:23. This was before the law was given to Moses and man was governed by his conscience. This was the period after Adam and Eve and extended through the Flood.

3. <u>The Dispensation of Promise</u> – Gen. 12:1-Ex. 19:8. This dispensation began with God's calling Abraham. God promised Abraham would father a great nation and that He would send the Messiah. (Gen. 12:1-3)

4. <u>The Dispensation of Law</u> – Ex. 19:8-Matt. 27:35. God began this dispensation when He freed the Hebrews under Moses' leadership and God them the Mosaic Law. During this period that covers most of the Old Testament God was revealing Himself through the Nation of Israel.

5. <u>The Dispensation of the Age of Principles</u> <u>(Also called the Age of Grace)</u> This It is often referred to as the Dispensation of

Grace. However, God has always extended grace to man and salvation through Jesus Christ as always by His grace. But today believers are not under the Law that God gave to the Nation of Israel. A church (ekklesia) is a voluntary assembly of believers who out of a love for Christ willing live according to God's principles. A church is not a governing body that has laws which they enforce as a nation does. Thus, in a biblical church God is working through His mercy and grace with individual believers who are free, having the liberty to live by the principles of God's word.

God commanded the Nation of Israel to obey the Ten Commandments and all the law He gave them to govern the nation. There were strict punishments for disobeying these nation laws the same as it is today in nation governments of nations.

It should be understood that the dispensation of the Old Testament is not finished. God postponed this dispensation when Israel rejected Jesus and crucified their Messiah. Daniel prophecies there would be 470 years to the coming of the Messiah and His kingdom. (Dan. 9:24-27)

Currently, 363 years of Daniel's prophecy have been fulfilled, leaving seven more years that are unfilled to God giving Israel their promised Kingdom. That seven years is the coming seven-year Tribulation. At the end of the seven-year Tribulation, Christ returns physically as promised in Acts 1:10-11. Fifty days later, Jesus will begin the one thousand years Millennium and fulfill His promise by establishing the kingdom to the Nation of Israel. (Rev. 20:5-6)

The Old Testament Law was not done away with, but fulfilled in Jesus Christ. (See Matt. 5:17) The Old Testament Law was a picture that foreshadowed the coming of Jesus the Messiah. Although believers today are not instructed to keep the Mosaic Law. The principles of the law are eternal principles are to be followed even though we are not told to keep the "letter" Law. (2 Cor. 3:6-11)

Paul explained this saying, "Wherefore the law was our schoolmaster to bring us unto Christ, that we might be justified by faith. But after that faith is come, we are no longer under a schoolmaster." (Galatians 3:24-25) In Romans, Paul reveals

"For sin shall not have dominion over you: for ye are not under the law, but

under grace. What then? shall we sin, because we are not under the law, but under grace? God forbid." (Romans 6:14-15.

Christians in our current dispensation follow the principle behind the Law, but not its details.

As stated earlier, a local church is not a nation and has no authority to execute laws. It is clear that Israel was a nation and the Law was their constitution and system of governmental laws. It is a serious error for Christians and churches in our dispensation to follow the Israel's system of government in keeping the feasts and specific ordnances given to Israel. I believe that most of the cults and false churches of today have made that error and degraded the Gospel and God's plan for believers in this age of liberty to willing obeying the principles of the Word of God. It honors our Savior when a believer willingly, apart from compulsion, lives a godly life

6. The Dispensation of the Millennial Kingdom. This is the period of one thousand years, in which God will give Israel the Kingdom He promised them in the Old Testament. All believers throughout all the ages will be a part of this world-wide Kingdom that Jesus will rule over from Jerusalem.

7. <u>The Dispensation of the New Heavens and Earth.</u> - Rev. 21-22. The is the last dispensation that last into eternality.

If one is to arrive at the correct meaning of a passage, you must consider when the statement was made in its historical, cultural, and dispensational context and further whom God was addressing. It is a gross error to ignore this hermeneutical rule. It is the author's estimate that ninety percent of false teaching comes from ignoring this biblical principle.

Applying Dispensational Truth in Interpretation

To understand the Mosaic Law properly, one must understand it was given in particular to the Nation Israel in the Old Testament dispensation of the Law and uniquely was applied to the Nation of Israel. The Mosaic Law was not given to Christians in this dispensation of the Age of Principles. Without question, God through the ages has worked with different people in different times in different ways. This is referred to as Dispensational Truth.

This article does not afford a sufficient medium to teach the Bible's dispensational truths. It is strongly suggested that any serious Bible student must study and fully comprehend Dispensational

Truth. A good source would be a Charles Ryrie's book "Dispensational Today."[13]

It is vital to understand who and how God was working with when interpreting the Bible. For example: When interpreting God's commands and laws in the Old Testament. God's law required Israel to stone false prophets as Deuteronomy 13:5 records. That is clearly what the passage says and what God commanded Israel to do and what was done following the Law. Israel was a nation and God gave them this instruction and authority to judge and to carry out capital punishment. Therefore, the proper interpretation of these laws is that Israel was to put false prophets to death and remove their sinful influence on the Hebrews.

How then we to understand that passage today? Today, as Christian assemblies, are we to follow the Mosaic Law and put false prophets to death? Obviously, we would not because we are not the Nation of Israel to whom the Law was given and we have no authority to execute such judgment. Israel was a nation under God's laws. We live in a different time in history, a different culture and different dispensation. Christians today are a different entity than Israel was centuries ago.

Another erroneous application of scripture that ignores dispensation truth is in the practice of some Christian groups worshiping on Saturday, the Sabbath Day. Exodus 31:12-17 specifically states the observance of the Sabbath was given by God to the Israelites. Nowhere in the Bible does God command believers in this Age to keep the Sabbath. It was not given to be an observance for Christians in this age. It was a special observance given to Israel to recognize God's covenant with them as His chosen people. It is not applicable to Christians in the Age of Principles. Christian churches worship on Sunday the first day of the week in honoring the day that Christ arose.

The Ten Commandments are in fact specific laws or commandments given to the nation of Israel. To violate one of these commandments would bring about a serious penalty and even death. Each of the commandments is based upon a biblical principle of conduct. Today we keep the principles of the Commandments, but are not required to keep the letter of the law, as in keeping Saturday as our day of worship. Christians worship on Sunday the first day of the week honoring Christ's resurrection.

We live in the dispensation of the Age of Principles sometimes called the Age of Grace.[14] I refer to it as the Age of Principles. God gave the Law to the Nation of Israel in a different dispensation called the Age of the Law. God gave the Law to the "Nation" of Israel; He did not give it to the Christians and churches. Paul said, The Mosaic Law was the Constitution, Bill of Rights and system of civil judicial laws for the nation of Israel. There is a vast difference between God given punishable laws to Israel as a nation in the Old Testament and Christians assembled in churches in the New Testament times. Churches are not a "nation" and do not have any political or civil authority over its members. Christians today meet voluntarily in the local assemblies made up of members of "like" faith. They willingly obey the Lord in the liberty of loving God and willingly living for Him.

Therefore, God was not addressing churches of today in Deuteronomy 13:5, and churches or Christians today have not been instructed to obey the specifics of the Mosaic Law. However, it is imperative to understand that each of God's laws to Israel was based on an eternal biblical and spiritual principles. We can learn from God's instructions, given to Israel, by recognizing the principles His laws are based on. As Paul stated the Law was a "schoolmaster" to teach Israel God's principles. (See Gal. 3:24-25) Christians can apply these principles on which the commandments were given. The law taught Israel spiritual principles and His truths. The law to stone false prophets and witches was given to keep the Hebrews separated from false teaching and its influence and to condemn the occult.

Christians today live by the principles on which these laws were based on by practicing biblical separation. "Wherefore come out from among them, and be ye separate, saith the Lord, and touch not the unclean *thing*; and I will receive you," (2 Corinthians 6:17) The Mosaic Law was valid in the Old Testament dispensation, but not valid for churches today in our dispensation. Clearly, it is plain that God worked differently with Israel as a nation than He works with Christians in assemblies today.

The churches of today live in a different economy. The word "dispensation" is the Greek word (*oikonomia*) and means an "economy," which signifies a stewardship, meaning the management or disposition of affairs in a particular time and to a particular people. "*Oikos*" is the word for house and "nomos" means law. Thus, the word means "the law of the house." Paul stated "That in the dispensation of the fulness of times he might gather together in one all things in Christ, both which are in heaven, and which are on earth; *even* in him:" (Ephesians 1:10) To the Corinthians he wrote:

> "For if I do this thing willingly, I have a reward: but if against my will, a dispensation of the gospel is

committed unto me." (1 Corinthians 9:17)

In Galatians 4:4 the phrase "*the fulness of the time*" (*to plêrôma tou chronou*), which refers to the time before Christ, is treated as a unit[15] showing God working in an exclusive way in a particular time with a specific people.

God is working differently with the churches than He did with Israel. However, we read the laws and apply the principles, do not follow false prophets or teachers keeping ourselves separated from the occult and such evil.

Christians today can apply the spiritual principles behind the Mosaic Laws by preaching and teaching God's truth correctly, denouncing false prophets, and remaining separated from them. It would be a wrong interpretation and application of the passage for Christians today to practice putting false prophets to death. That would be a grave historical and dispensational blunder.

CHAPTER THREE
Interpreting Considering the Historical Setting

Another example is seen in understanding the historical setting of the Book of Daniel, which is vital in interpreting that Book. In interpreting the Book of Daniel, one must consider that Daniel was a captive in Babylon in 527 B.C. All the events of his life from his youth being taken into captivity into his old age took place in Babylon. This historical information would be essential in understanding the Book of Daniel.

Another example of ignoring the historical setting of a passage that would be confusing is the use of the names "Judah" and "Israel." Historically, the twelve tribes of Jacob were called the Nation of Israel. However, the twelve tribes of Israel divided after the death of King Solomon when his son Rehoboam came to the throne. Being a wicked tyrant, the ten northern refused to follow him. The tribes, Judah and Benjamin followed Rehoboam establishes the southern nation of Judah. The ten northern tribes retained the name Israel.

Prior to the death of Solomon, all the tribes bore the name Israel. However, after Solomon, the kingdom was divided and the ten tribes, that occupied the northern area of the Promised Land, were called Israel. During this period, the southern tribes of Judah and Benjamin were called Judah. Both Israel and Judah had their own kings and at times warred against each other. It is necessary to understand that once the Nation of Israel divided the names "Israel" and "Judah" then identified the two nations that were once simply Israel.

Generally, the name "Israel" is referring to the nation as a whole or the twelve tribes. However, other times it refers only to the ten northern tribes after the tribes separated after Solomon's death. Likewise, the name "Judah" can refer to the Southern Kingdom (the two tribes of Judah and Benjamin), or it may be referred to Judah alone. You must consider the historical setting of the word's use to know to whom it refers.

Another example of the importance of history in interpretation is that often the name Edom has been misunderstood. Esau was Isaac's oldest son and the brother of Jacob. Esau sold his birthright to Jacob for a bowl of pottage, and since then he was also called Edom. (Gen. 25:30) Esau married a Canaanite woman and settled in Seri, which is in southern Jordan. This land was named after Esau and called Edom. Edom therefore referred to Esau, to the land he settled, and to his descendants. Edom was the bitter enemy of Israel. Over four hundred years later when Moses sought to lead the Children of Israel through the land of Edom, but the Edomites refused them passage. Therefore, God condemned Edom, and predicted that Edom would become a wasteland and all the Edomites would be destroyed, which is what happened. Therefore, when reading the Old Testament, it is vital to know to whom and in what time the name Edom referred.

Cultural Errors

The oriental or Eastern marriage is completely different from the occidental marriages of Western civilization. Marriages in the eastern culture were arranged by the fathers of the bride and groom. In pre-Mosaic times, when the families agreed to the marriage a proposal price was given and the bridegroom could come at once and take away his bride to his own house (Gen. 24:63-67). Later, this was changed and the first stage of an oriental marriage was the betrothal in which a friend of the bridegroom or his parents presented the proposal to the family of the bride. If the proposal was accepted, there was a period of time between the betrothal and the next event, which would be the wedding ceremony. When the proposal was accepted the bride was considered married. (Matt. 1:19, John 3:29) At a later time, the bridegroom would come to the home of the bride and the bride's family would put on a feast. During the feast, the bridegroom would take his bride to his home the bridal chamber and consummate the marriage. To understand oriental marriage is vital to understand the parable of the virgins in Matthew 25, or to understand the "marriage supper of the Lamb" (Rev. 19:9). If biblical marriage is interpreted applying the practices of the Western or occidental marriage one would arrive at an erroneous understanding.

Interpreting the Parable of the Ten Virgins

Understanding marriage in Eastern culture helps interpret the many passages in the New Testament that refer to marriage and Eastern marriage customs. Jesus in Matthew 25 said the kingdom of heaven is likened to ten virgins who took their lamp to meet the bridegroom. Five virgins went prepared with extra oil for their lamp and patiently waited for the arrival of the bridegroom. The other five were unprepared, taking no additional oil, and when the bridegroom's arrival was announced, they tried to get oil from the five prepared virgins but were refused. They went out to purchase more oil, but when they returned the bridegroom had already arrived and they were not allowed to attend the wedding feast.

Understanding the marriage culture during Bible times lets us properly interpret Jesus' parable that revealed truth about Christ's Second Coming. The parable of the ten virgins was used by God to illustrate Jesus the Christ coming and taking His bride at His Second Coming. The virgins were not the bride, which is Christians who make up the Body of Christ. The ten virgins, representing Israel, were invited to the wedding supper. Five of the virgins were looking for the Bridegroom to arrive and were prepared to receive Him. Five foolish virgins were not ready and left to get oil for their lamps that had run out. The interpretation is literally the details of the account as Jesus revealed it. The context of the passage is plainly near the end of the seven-year Tribulation, thus the application of the parable illustrates the simple truth that Jesus was warning Israel to be prepared for His Second Coming. It would be a serious error to try interjecting western marriage customs in interpreting marriage in the Old Testament that would confuse the application. To allegorize any portion of the parable would only produce a false interpretation. Parables have only one interpretation and should never be spiritualized.

Paul's Instructions For Women to Cover Their Heads When Praying

Another passage is that the culture of New

Testament times explains is 1 Corinthians 11:4-5. The passage is Paul explaining that women were to cover their heads when praying. This was the cultural custom of the time.

> *"Every man praying or prophesying, having his head covered, dishonoureth his head. But every woman that prayeth or prophesieth with her head uncovered dishonoureth her head: for that is even all one as if she were shaven." (1 Corinthians 11:4-5)*

In Jewish culture, the man would cover his head when praying with his *tallith*.[16] A *tallith* is a shawl that has knotted fringes at each of its four corners and is worn by Jewish men when they prayed. It is worn to show humility before Almighty God. The Greek custom was to pray with the head uncovered. It seems that Paul chose to follow the Gentile custom based on Christ's incarnation as a man. A male believer, then being in Christ could stand unveiled in the presence of his Lord and Master. Further, in oriental society, the head covering could also illustrate mourning. Therefore, a man praying without his head covered honored God the Father and was done with joy.

In Eastern culture, a woman was to wear a veil or head covering when in public. Paul explains the reason in 1 Corinthians 11:7,

"For a man indeed ought not to cover his head, forasmuch as he is the image and glory of God: but the woman is the glory of the man."

The wearing of a headdress by a woman honored her husband and acknowledged his God given responsibility as the head of his family. It would be a serious breach of etiquette for a woman to go into the public without her headdress. In doing so, she would dishonor herself and her husband and if done when praying it would also dishonor the Lord. Further, in their culture it was an act of rebellion for a woman to go unveiled. In verse 6, Paul compared the shame for an uncovered woman in their society on equal status with a disobedient slave girl or an adulteress that was punished by shaving her head. Therefore, because of their culture, Paul instructed godly Christian women to show their respect for God, their husband, and themselves to pray with their heads covered.

The question then arises, should modern Christians women wear head covering when they pray in public? The answer is simple and rests with one's culture. If a woman today is in the Middle East in a culture where women cover their heads, they should follow the custom. If a woman is in a Western culture where women do not cover their heads, then they are under no obligation to wear a veil. In Western culture, whether a woman wears a head covering or not is not an issue and the practice is not related to her showing respect for God or their husband.

The interpretation of the passage is clear in instruction as to Christian women in Eastern culture covering their heads in public and when praying. However, it is plain that this was a cultural admonishment and not applicable in every society.

Make Christ Central In All Interpretations

In John 5:38, Jesus said, "Search the Scriptures for in them ye think ye have eternal life: and they are they that speak of me." The whole Bible is about the Lord Jesus Christ, the Messiah. Christ is the central theme in all Scripture. An example of not taking this principle into consideration would be to say that God had a plan of salvation in the Old Testament, but in the New Testament Christ has a new plan. Some have mistakenly concluded that in the Old Testament saints were saved by the Law or works and in the New Testament by Grace. However, salvation from the beginning of time has not changed. Ephesians 2:7-9 is a universal passage of scripture applicable in all ages. "That in the ages to come he might shew the exceeding riches of his grace in his kindness toward us through Christ Jesus. For by grace are ye saved through faith; and that not of yourselves: it is the gift of God: Not of works, lest any man should boast." (Ephesians 2:7-9) (Also, see Romans 5)

The Book of Hebrews clearly says that the Law and all the sacrifices did not atone for sin. Hebrews 11, states the all the Old Testament saints through faith, received the promises of God. Their faith was in the future coming of the Messiah and Savior who would atone for sin. Thus, Christ was central in salvation, in the Old Testament as He is in the New Testament. It was Christ's death on the Cross that saved the Old Testament saints. They believed and accepted God's promise of the Messiah by faith. They trusted in Him as their coming Messiah, before the fact of His birth, death, burial and resurrection. They believed God and were saved by faith in the truth that God had given them at that time. Therefore, they were saved by God's grace, through faith just like all believers throughout all the ages. The Old Testament believers were looking forward to the coming of the Messiah. In our day we look back. It was the faith in God's promises that saved them. The Old Testament believers trusted in the Lord and kept rituals and the Law in obedience because they believed.

Keeping the Law never saved anyone and proof of this was in that New Testament records many like the rich ruler who came to Jesus asking what could he do to inherit eternal life? (Mark 10:17-23) He said he had kept the Law since his youth. Jesus told him that he lacked one thing. He told him to sell what he had and give to the poor and to take up the cross and follow Him. The rich ruler went away lost because even though he had kept the Law, he would not put his faith in Jesus. Those that teach salvation was different in the Old Testament than in our present age are in serious error.

Jesus appeared many times throughout the Old Testament. He was in the Garden of Eden and communed with Adam and Eve. He is recorded as appearing and is called the Angel of the Lord. In the Old Testament, Jesus' appearances are referred to as a "Theophany"[17] or "Christophanies."[18] These were all pre-incarnate appearances of Christ. The title "Angel of the Lord" occurs 52 times in the Old Testament and 27 times the appearance of the Lord is recorded by the phrase "the LORD appeared."

In Exodus 3:2, the name "Angel of the Lord" refers to Jesus Christ who appeared to Moses in the bushing bush. Verse 4 confirms this saying that the Lord, "Jehovah" saw that Moses turned aside to see the burning bush, "And when the

LORD (Jehovah) saw that he turned aside to see, God (Elohiyam) called unto him out of the midst of the bush. . ." (Exodus 3:4)

The word translated in our English Bibles "LORD" is the Hebrew word "Jehovah." The significance of this truth is that Jesus, their Messiah, had appeared many times to Israel prior to His incarnation. Regretfully, their sinful hearts blinded them to the One they had been speaking to them and they were expecting for 2000 years.

Thus, the theme of God's word is Jesus Christ, God's son who came to give Himself as a sacrifice to pay the sin debt of the whole world throughout all time, Old or New Testament.

> *"For God so loved the world, that he gave his only begotten Son, that whosoever believeth in him should not perish, but have everlasting life." (John 3:16)*

> *"But when the fulness of the time was come, God sent forth his Son, made of a woman, made under the law, To redeem them that were under the law, that we might receive the adoption of sons." (Galatians 4:4-5)*

CHAPTER FOUR
Be Conscious of Context

The context of a text or verse refers to its setting within a larger portion of Scripture. It is vital that a word, or passage be interpreted within its context. To ignore the context of a passage will almost always lead to an erroneous interpretation.

It refers to the verses or statements that occur before and after the text. This would include the paragraph, chapter and book or the whole of the Bible. The situation surrounding the text is relevant in understanding its meaning. The writers of Scripture wrote in the environment in which they lived and this is why knowing the background, culture and current situation of a scripture passage is so important. This is why the Historical, Cultural, Grammatical method of interpretation is the only biblical way to determine God's meaning. Further, the writers were being inspired by God to present biblical truth. This truth is learned *"line upon line, precept upon precept"* and therefore the correct interpretation of a verse or phrase is absolutely dependent on the whole of the context in which it is stated. (Isa. 28:10)

For an example, look at 1 Corinthians 15:32: The verse ends with the words, *". . . Let us eat, drink for tomorrow we die."* If quoted without considering the context of this phrase or quoted by itself would appear to be saying that Paul was teaching a person is to live a carefree life, eating and drinking, getting all the "gusto" they can. A look at the context of the statement shows that Paul was teaching quite the opposite. The statement is a reference to worldly philosophy that one only lives for the moment and ignores the future. Paul was instructing the Corinthians that there is certainly life after death and that man will be judged and held accountable for his deeds. The point Paul made was that if there was no resurrection of the dead, there was no reason to live a righteous life. In verse 34, Paul is rebuking the Corinthians for the way they were living "eating and drinking" without any regard for the coming resurrection and judgment. They were living as if there was not going to be a resurrection and this was to their shame! Therefore, we see that the context of a verse is very important and absolutely necessary for understanding or interpreting the verse.

The false teachings and beliefs, that are so prevalent today, can be traced to ignoring the context of a passage. Mistakes can be made by sincere men, but other times false teachers, who have no fear of God, deliberately deceive their followers for their personal gain.

The Mormons quote 1 Corinthians 15:29, as their text verse in establishing their practice of baptizing the living for the dead. However, the context reveals the true interpretation. The subject of the whole chapter of 1 Corinthians 15 is the resurrection. The chapter presents the truth of the resurrection. Paul in making this statement was not teaching a doctrine. He was using the practice of some pagan religions of baptizing for the dead as an illustration of the universal belief in life after death. How do we know that this is what he meant? Look at the context of the statement. From the context of the statement, we can see that the subject of the chapter and the passage is the resurrection of the dead. Verse 12, establishes the theme and subject Paul is addressing, "Now if Christ be preached that he rose from the dead, how say some among you that there is no resurrection of the dead." Contextually, verse 29 is a part of Paul's answer to this question. You cannot honestly say what this verse means without considering the context and everything said in conjunction to this statement. The Bible nowhere teaches that baptisms for the dead are a Christian practice or Biblical doctrine. This is the only reference to such a practice in the Bible and there is no biblical or extra biblical record of Christians ever baptizing for the dead.

Note what Paul said, "Else what shall they do which are baptized for the dead, if the dead rise not at all? why are they then baptized for the dead?" (1 Corinthians 15:29) The "they" of the verse cannot be referring to Christians, but someone other than Christians. Actually, pagans who practiced this unbiblical practice, but did believe in the resurrection of the dead.

1. The following statement illustrates the importance of context in understanding what a statement means or its interpretation:

"If the Egyptians (pagans) did not believe in life after death, why did they go to such great lengths in preparing their dead for the hereafter?"

2. In making this statement, one would not be establishing the validity of their practices in preparing the dead for the afterlife, but merely noting it. The validity of life after death is not being addressed. Their practice of baptizing for the dead showed their belief. There is no hint in the statement that the person condoned the practices of the Egyptians. The point the writer is making is that pagans believed in an afterlife because of how they prepared their dead. Likewise, Paul was not establishing a doctrine or telling

the Corinthians to do this. He does not even say that they were doing this. He said the pagans were the ones who baptized for the dead. Nevertheless, he knew they were aware of pagan religions that did baptize for the death. He then referred to something that was known to them and used the practice as an illustration of the universal belief in life after death even among most non-believers. The statement cannot be correctly understood if you do not take into consideration the context in which the statement was made. He absolutely was not teaching that Christians are to be baptized for dead people. Baptism is a ritual in which a believer proclaims his faith in Jesus Christ and is a public declaration of his new birth.

3. Let's look at another example of the importance of the context of a statement in the following:

"Police today arrested, Bill Smith for the murder of his wife Jane Smith. The Police reported that Bill Smith later changed his story. In an earlier statement, Bill claimed that John Doe had murdered Bill's wife. Bill now has made a full confession."

Suppose in reading this statement to you someone would only read the partial statement: "John Doe murdered Bill's wife." This statement by itself would lead you to believe John Doe had murdered his wife. However, if you read the whole paragraph you would see that this was not what the article meant at all.

You can see in this illustration the importance of the context of a statement. Context helps determine what happened, and what is the correct interpretation of the written statement.

4. The established rule is, "A text without a context is only a pretext."[19] The definition of the word "pretext" means a false reason or motive put forth to hide the real one. It is impossible to understand the meaning of any statement without considering its context.

We must consider the following aspects of context in researching a passage.

Examining a Passage in the Various Forms of Context

Context falls into several different relations or frames of reference. There are the Immediate, Broad, Parallel, Historical, Cultural, and Analogical Context.

1. The Immediate Context of the verse means the verses just before and after the verse.

2. The Broad Context of a verse addresses the verse's place within the chapter and the entire book.

3. The Parallel Context of the verse refers to other places the word or text is found. It may be in the same book or a different place in Scripture.

4. The Historical Context addresses the time in history the passage is revealing and its culture. The geological and political situation could also reveal a great deal about the interpretation.

5. The Cultural Context considers both the common and unique cultural practices in which the passage was written and to which it applies.

6. The Analogical Context reveals the relationship with the passage and the other teachings of God's word.

The Immediate Context

The Immediate Context of John 3:16 would be then shown in reading from verses 1 to 36. Although the truth of Christ's statement stands by its self, the statements Jesus made before and after verse 16 enrich our understand God's plan of salvation and help us to interpret His statements. In understanding John 3:16 it would be considered that Jesus was talking with Nicodemus, a Pharisee who was seeking to learn who Jesus truly was considering His message and miracles.

In verse 3 the Lord explained to him that he must be born again and to inherit the kingdom of heaven. Nicodemus already thought that being a Jew and religious, he would inherit the kingdom of heaven. Jesus explained, "Verily, verily, I say unto thee, Except a man be born of water and of the Spirit, he cannot enter into the kingdom of God. That which is born of the flesh is flesh; and that which is born of the Spirit is spirit." (John 3:5-6) When Jesus said that God sent His son that "whosoever" believeth in Him should not perish, He was telling Nicodemus two things: One, God's love extended to the whole world and; two, salvation was through belief. In verse 13, Jesus confirmed that He was the Messiah who came down from heaven. Thus, the context explains fully what Jesus meant.

Many want to interpret John 3:5, as referring to baptism, "Jesus answered, Verily, verily, I say unto thee, Except a man be born of water and *of* the Spirit, he cannot enter into the kingdom of God" to baptism. The context corrects that error. Jesus continued and stated "That which is born of the flesh is flesh; and that which is born of the Spirit is spirit." (John 3:6) No one is born of the Spirit by baptism. Many passages clearly teach that works, ritual or anything else does not save, and that salvation by faith in Jesus Christ is God's

only plan of salvation. (See Eph. 2:8-9; <u>Rom.
3:20,27-28</u>; <u>4:2</u>; <u>9:11,16</u>; <u>11:6</u>; <u>1 Cor. 1:29-31</u>; <u>2
Tim. 1:9</u>; <u>Titus 3:3-5</u>) Jesus is saying that man is
born in the flesh was referring to Nicodemus'
Hebrew birth and that it would not save him. He
said only spiritual birth, of the Holy Spirit, could
save. The context of the verse is clearly teaching
that spiritual birth saves, not water baptism.

The Broad Context

The Broad Context establishes the passage's
place in the chapter, book, and New Testament.
For example the Broach Context of Galatians 1
would include who the Galatians were, why was
Paul writing the Epistle to them, and would explain
his pointed statement of verses 8-9 stating that if
anyone ". . . preach any other gospel unto you
than that which we have preached unto you, let
him be **accursed**" meaning ". . . devoted for
destruction."[20] The context of verses 6-7 explains
that the Galatians had abandoned the truth Paul
had taught them, and were accepting a different
Gospel from the Gospel of Christ. Verse 13
identifies the false teachers as Jews who were
teaching Christians were to practice the Mosaic
Law. He states his credentials as being a learned
and devout Jew who had been saved and was
teaching what he received from Christ and not
Judaism. The Board Context would consider the

whole of Paul's message in this letter.

The Parallel Context

An example of studying a Parallel Context in the Gospels would be accomplished by consulting a "Harmony of the Gospels" to find other Scriptures where the accounts of an event in the life of Christ are found.

Another application of studying the Parallel Context is that if the New Testament quotes an Old Testament passage. Research of the subject of the passage would include its context and interpretation in the Old Testament passages as well. This would add insight into the meaning of both the New Testament and Old Testament passages. It would help you understand why the New Testament writer quoted it and what it means.

For an example in the Synoptic Gospels, you will find three accounts of the Temptation of Christ. (Matt. 4:1-11, Mark 1:12-13, and Luke 4:1-13) Seeking a Parallel Context could give a greater understanding of the event, as one writer may give information another would omit. Further, each of the Gospels was written for a particular audience. Matthew was written to the Jews; Mark to the Romans; and Luke to the Gentiles. Reading and studying each account from these three perspectives would aid one in understanding a single event.

Above we listed a number of references that proclaim that works do not save and that it is faith which is a gift of God that saves. These are parallel references that teach the same truth.

The Historical Context

Seeking the Historical Context would lead to consulting history to find the setting of the statement. The Historical Context can be found from several places. First would be the historical background of the Book that the passage of Scripture is found. Who wrote the passage, when was it written, to whom was it written, and what was it about. A secular account of the history of that period could add a great deal to your understanding of the period. Next, you could consult one or several of Bible studies helps or reference works. Books on archaeological discoveries made in the Bible lands have shed light on many Biblical events. All these findings together would show the current traditions or political situations of the passage. Language studies will show how a word was used in the past and help reveal what was its original meaning and usage. A Bible dictionary or commentary could also provide information as to the historical context.

In studying the Book of Daniel, it is important

to research the history surrounding Daniel's life, Babylon, Persia, and of Israel in captivity. It is greatly revealing to understand Israel's history during the life of Christ and the First Century. Thus, knowing the historical times in the First Century would keep a student from interpreting biblical events and applying Western culture.

The Cultural Context

Each book of the Bible was written within a specific period in history. For example, each of the Epistles in the New Testament was written to a different church in a particular geographical location. Each church was unique due to the culture it existed in. For example, the cultural and historical Context of the Galatians would reveal who the Galatians were and details about their city and country. A good Bible dictionary or handbook would reveal the particularities of the city where the church was located and the cultural influence that location was reflected in that congregation. It would show they were a mixed church of Jews and Gentiles who lived in a Roman colony in Asia Minor. Research would show they were a proud, even boastful, and independent people who, after accepting the Gospel, they changed very quickly to a new form of religion, not from fickleness, but from a certain proneness to a more oriental form of religion with rituals.[21] Judaism provided them rituals that biblical Christianity did not. The Cultural Context would better explain why they were susceptible to abandoning the true Gospel, and accepting a form of Judaism. This information would help a student reach an accurate interpretation of the Book and shed important light on the situation there.

A bible student must research each city, providence, or country to get a greater insight into Paul's Epistles. The subjects Paul addressed in the New Testament are vital to understand his concentrating on various problems in each of these earlier churches. Some of Paul's statements or admonishments were cultural such as requiring women to cover their heads and men to go bareheaded. (See 1 Cor. 11:6-7) Understanding the culture of his day shows us that the practice is not applicable today and modern Christians live in a different culture.

The Analogical Context

The Analogical Context is vital to arriving at the proper interpretation of a passage of Scripture. An analogy in scripture is a comparison between passages in the Bible, which address the same or a similar subject often from a different perspective. It is similar to the parallel context. The purpose is to seek an explanation or clarification, or continuity of the subject.

The analogy of a passage of Scripture deals with its resemblance or similarity with the rest of the Bible. This is discussed in detail in the next section. Briefly, it means that Scripture does not contradict itself. If the passage you read seems to contradict some other Scripture, then you must study further to understand the passage to be able to resolve the seeming conflict. Further, if one arrives at an interpretation which is in conflict with other scriptures the interpretation is false. God's word the Bible is truth and truth does not contradict itself. All of the scriptures are truth without error.

An example of the analogy clarifying a passage of scripture is Matthew 13:13, "And ye shall be hated of all *men* for my name's sake: but he that shall endure unto the end, the same shall be saved." (Mark 13:13) Some mistakenly state this verse teaches a works salvation in that a believer must "endure to the end" in order to be saved. The context of Jesus' statement is at the end the seven-year Tribulation and Christ's Second Coming. Those Jesus is addressing, are those believers who somehow remain alive until His return at the end of the seven years during this catastrophic period when God is judging the earth.

Note Mathew 13:20, "And except that the Lord had shortened those days, no flesh should be saved: but for the elect's sake, whom he hath chosen, he hath shortened the days." (Mark 13:20) The scriptures do not teach that believers must "endure to the end" to be saved. Considering 1 Peter 1:5 that states," Who are kept by the power of God through faith unto salvation ready to be revealed in the last time." (1 Peter 1:5) A believer receives eternal life when he believers in Jesus Christ and cannot lose his salvation. The false idea is that Jesus made the down payment or our salvation, but we must keep up the payments (good works) until we die to be saved. This an many other passages of God's word teaches us that "once saved, always saved."

CHAPTER FIVE

The Error of Ignoring Sound Principles of Interpretation

For example, the great error today of the Pentecostal and Charismatic movements of today is that they ignore the context of what the New Testament says about speaking in unlearned languages (tongues). They fail to see the historical setting of Acts 2 and what God truly did on that day. They also ignore 1 Corinthians 13:8-10, which emphatically states that when the Bible was complete "tongues "would cease and therefore ignore the broad context of this early church sign gift and other passages that show the error in modern "tongues."

The Pre-wrath Rapture proponents, Reformers, cults, and the Amillennialists ignore the dispensational truths concerning God's plan for the Jews and mix up promises and prophecies concerning Israel with God' plan for the institution of the local church. The result of such careless hermeneutics has produced untold confusion and division. Those with unsound principles of interpretation are insubstantial and immature.

The sincere seeker of God's truth must be diligent in his studies. It is truly sinful to refuse to study and to apply God's rules of interpretation. To incorrectly interpret a passage of Scripture is to add or subtract from God's word and is condemned by God. Jesus Christ is the *"Logos"* meaning "the word of God. You cannot separate Christ from the Word as they are One and the same. Jesus Christ as John 1:1 says is the Word. To tamper with or misuse the Word of God is to defame Christ Himself and instead of teachings God's truth, present lies as being the truth. That is a serious error and thus it is vital and absolutely necessary to know what God actually meant by what He said. The task of hermeneutics is to arrive correctly at presenting an accurate interpretation of what God said. How easily those who do not read, studying God's word can be misled.

Every Scripture is interconnected to all other Scriptures. You cannot take a verse or passage out of its context, away from the other Scriptures and interpret it correctly. This leads us to the next principle of interpretation.

Interpret by the Analogy of the Faith

The Bible does not contradict itself and God did not make the Bible to be contradictory. If a passage of Scripture seems to contradict some other scripture, the problem is not with the Bible, but with the interpreter.

Some may object to the premise that the Bible does not contradict itself. However, at the heart of understanding the Bible is understanding of two truths. One infallible truth is that God is Omniscience and knows all things. He cannot contradict Himself, because it is not in His nature to do so. God cannot lie and if even one scripture conflicted or made a paradoxical statement, then one of the statements would be false and thus a lie. God cannot lie as God is without question Truth.

The Bible claims to be the Very Word of God! To attack and discredit the Bible is to attack and discredit God. God is totally capable of giving us this revelation accurately and did so when He inspired each word, paragraph, chapter, and book of the Bible. God's truth certainly does not rest on a fallible man. God gave us His method of interpretation in letting Him interpret His word.

Inspiration and Interpretation

The term "inspiration" is the theological term that expresses the truth that the Bible given by God is His every word without error. Let us go over this again. To understand inspiration, we must look at two classic Scripture verses:

The first passage is 2 Tim. 3:16-17 "All scripture is given by inspiration of God, and is profitable for doctrine, for reproof, for correction, for instruction in righteousness: That the man of God may be perfect, throughly furnished unto all good works." (2 Timothy 3:16-17)

The word "inspiration" is literally interpreted "God-breathed." The Greek word is *"theopneutos"*, which means *"theo"* = God, and *"pneutos"* = breathed. The Hebrew word is *"nehemiah"* and is used only once in the Old Testament in Job 32:8. The verse is saying God breathed on the writers of the Bible and they wrote His Very Word. In other words, God superintended the writing of the Bible so that the author was God Himself and the writer wrote exactly word for word what God intended. God used these men to pen the Bible, but what they wrote did not come from themselves and relying on their intelligence, wisdom, or insight.

The next passage is 2 Peter 1:21, "For prophecy came not in old times by the will of man but holy men of God spoke as they were moved by the Holy Spirit."

Literally, the verse is confirming 2 Timothy 3:16-17, that inspiration is the process by which the Holy Spirit supernaturally moved on the writers of Scripture and what they wrote was not their words, but the very word of God. God superintended each and every word of Scripture and they accurately reflect what He intended to say. Hebrews 1:1 says, "God, who at sundry times and in divers manners spoke in time past unto our fathers." Therefore, God has at different times in the past, and in many ways has spoken through men to reveal Himself to mankind. Paul and Peter state that what these men wrote was God's word.

Examples of how God spoke to man or revealed Himself and His will. Hosea 12:10 "I have also spoken by the prophets, and have multiplied visions, and used similitudes, by the ministry of the prophets." A literal translation of the verse says, "I spoke to the prophets, gave them many visions."

1. God spoke by angels to Abraham and Lot in Genesis 18-19. To Daniel, in Dan. 10:10-21.
2. In visions as Isaiah 1:1; Ezekiel 1:1; 8:3, 11:24, 43:3; Daniel 7:1, 8:1, 10:1 reveal.
3. By miracles. Exodus 3:2, Moses and the burning bush. Judges 6:37-39, Gideon's wool fleece.
4. By voice directly. Exodus 19, to Moses, I Samuel 3, to young Samuel.
5. Through an inner voice. Jer. 46:1-6. By casting lots. Jonah 1:7, Prov. 16:33.

David said, "The spirit of the Lord spake by me and his word was in my tongue" (2 Sam. 23:2). God used men to speak to other men. When the prophets spoke what God had revealed to them, they used phrases such as "thus saith the Lord", or "the Word of God came to me saying." They made it clear that what they were saying was from God.

To look at the matter in a practical way, what was happening was that as the writer sat down and wrote, God directed what they wrote. In 2 Peter 1:21, the words "moved on him" (*phero*) means "to bear, or carry, in 2 Peter 1:21, signifying that they were "borne along," or impelled by the Holy Spirit's power, not acting according to their wills, or simply expressing their own thoughts, but expressing the mind of God in words provided and ministered by Him."[22] Their wills were only involved in that they were willing instruments of God's will. As writers wrote, the Spirit guided their thoughts so that what they produced was from God without error or omission. It was, literally, exactly, word for word, what God wanted written

In theological terms, the doctrine that God wrote the Scriptures and that every word of Scripture is inspired of God is called, "verbal plenary inspiration." This is the view of Scripture that the Bible itself teaches.

1. Definitions of the words are: VERBAL = "WORDS" and PLENARY = "FULL." It means that God-breathed the very word of God in full expression of His thoughts in what the writer of Scripture wrote. This means that every word that was written was the mind of God without error. In other words, although the Bible was penned by men, it was really God who is the author.

2. God guided them in the choice of every word and expression. This does not mean God did not allow for personality and cultural background

of the writer to be used in expressing God's Words. God allowed the writers to express His thoughts in their own way. The books of the Bible show distinct characteristics of the men God used to pen the documents. For example, the writing of Paul shows a particular writing style that was different from the other writers.

3. This is why we must conclude the Bible is without error or contradiction. God wrote His word and preserves it, and not man. It is the product of God, and His very Word to man. It then is without error or contradiction.

4. When there seems to be an error or contradiction, the problem is in the interpretation of the verse or passage not the Scriptures. If your passage appears to be a contradiction, then your course of action is to continue studying until you arrive at the correct interpretation that will not be in conflict with other scripture. Often, arriving at the correct interpretation of a passage of Scripture will take a great deal of study.

CHAPTER SIX

Applying the Principles of Biblical Interpretation

Let us look at one "so called" problem passage. 1 Peter 3:19 says, "By which also "He" (referring to Christ) went and preached unto the spirits in prison." At first, reading the verse appears to say that Christ after His crucifixion went into Hell and preached salvation to the lost pre-flood peoples giving them a second chance for salvation.

This presents the interpreter of Scripture with a serious problem because other Scriptures clearly state man does not have a second chance to be saved. After death comes a man's judgment.

Job 21:30, states the "The wicked is "reserved" to the day of destruction." Hebrews 9:27 explains that "It is appointed unto men once to die, but after this the judgment." In Luke 16:22, the rich man in Hell, begs for mercy, but was denied even a drop of water.

If you consider these verses in the analogy of the faith, saying that this verse teaches that Jesus gave those who lived before the flood a second chance is a contradiction of other Scriptures. This alerts you to the problem! In considering, what the verse means you must consider the analogy of the faith. In other words, does this interpretation contradict other Scripture? Clearly, concluding that the antediluvian (prediluvian) were given a second chance for salvation is a contradiction, so you would be alerted to look for another correct meaning. The next step to resolve the problem would be to take into consideration the other principles of interpretation. Using these principles, you attempt to arrive at an interpretation that is not contradictory. The principle of interpreting within a verse's context would lead to you to read the verses before and after this one. The context of the verse would show you that Peter is writing about Christ's suffering and death for the sins of the world. This is the subject of these verses. (See verse 18) Verse 20, gives us the time of the preaching to the pre-flood people. It says, "When once the long-suffering of God, waited in the days of Noah." Therefore, the verse tells us this preaching was done in the days of Noah, not at the death of the Lord Jesus.

From the passage, the explanation becomes clear. The pre-flood people were offered salvation, by Noah, who preached to them before the flood. The principle, that we are to make Christ central to the Scriptures, points us to understand Christ made possible the salvation that God offered to the pre-flood people. Noah, in preaching salvation was preaching Christ! The "spirits" or the pre-

Flood people who rejected Noah's warning and offer of redemption are in "prison" (Hades) awaiting the judgment of Revelation 20:11-15. This interpretation does not violate any doctrine of Scripture and is not contradictory. It then is the best and correct interpretation. You see then that we are letting the Scriptures interpret the Scriptures.

The rule is a simple one: In interpreting, the Scriptures you must always consider the fact that the Bible does not contradict itself. If a proposed interpretation conflicts with other Scripture, then your interpretation is not correct. You then must continue your study and arrive at an interpretation that is not contradictory and in line with the rest of scripture.

Recognize the Progress of Revelation

In the proper interpretation of Scripture, it must be understood that God gave His revelation, the Bible, to man over many centuries. This is the doctrine of "Progressive Revelation." For an example, when God gave the first prophecy of the coming of Christ, He revealed very few of the details. God only revealed that, "I will put enmity between thy seed and her seed it shall bruise thy head, and thou shalt bruise his heel." (Genesis 3:15) All Adam and Eve knew was that God was promising them a Redeemer, who would overcome Satan and bring an end to the curse caused by their sin. God, then progressively revealed His Plan of Salvation over the whole period of the Old Testament. Over time, as God worked with man, He revealed more about the Messiah and gave more details. Those before Abraham knew nothing of God's plan to make of the Patriarch a great nation from whom the Messiah would come. Abraham only knew God's Messianic promise to: "And I will make of thee a great nation, and I will bless thee, and make thy name great; and thou shalt be a blessing: And I will bless them that bless thee, and curse him that curseth thee: and in thee shall all families of the earth be blessed." (Genesis 12:2-3) He knew nothing about how God would use his son's Isaac and Jacob (Israel) nor of Moses and the Law. God progressively revealed and brought these things into existence over hundreds of years. David knew of the coming of the Messiah, but did not know His name. To David and Isaiah, God revealed the Messiah would suffer for man's sins. (Psa. 22, Isa. 53) Four hundred years before Christ's coming, the Old Testament was completed and God had revealed, the Savior's name (Immanuel), place of birth, that He would be from the tribe of Judah, year of birth, that His death would atone for sins, the virgin birth and a total of over 300 prophecies concerning Christ's coming.

Consider that Abraham, the Father of the Nation of Israel, died having never heard of the nation Israel or the Law. When Israel became a nation and needed laws to govern them, over four hundred years later, God used Moses and gave him the Law at Mt. Sinai for Israel. The Law given was the "Constitution" of the Nation of Israel. It sets forth principles and specific instructions as to what was right and wrong in all spiritual and civil matters. It sets penalties for crimes against God and individual Israelites. God made them special ordinances such as the Sabbath, circumcision, the Temple, and a host of other things uniquely to Israel. The Mosaic Law addressed everything from cleanliness to relations with other nations. God had not earlier revealed these things. No one from Adam to Moses knew of God's specific Laws. They knew God had promised a Messiah and in faith, they accepted the revelation the Lord had given them up to that time.

We live now in the Dispensation popularly called the Age of Grace (Eph. 3:2). The author likes to call this the Age of Principles. Christians are not under the Old Testament law. (Rom. 6:14) Christians live by a higher rule, that being the principles of God. We have the liberty to obey God out of love and are not under a national civil law to obey God as was the Hebrews, where violations brought punishment. The law defined right, wrong, and commanded men to do what is right. However, you do not have to command people to do right when they believe God and that is what they want to do. When God gave commandments, they were given to define correct actions.

When the Old Testament Laws were broken by the Israelites, the priests administered justice. In the Age of Principles, every believer is indwelt by the Spirit of God who brings conviction. We have the Word of God to instruct us in righteousness. When we sin, the Holy Spirit convicts us and God chastens each believer who refuses to repent or wills to remain in sin. (Heb. 12:6-11) No civil authority or church has that right or authority in this age to exact punishment in our age. Our civil government does not punish us when we disobey God's commandments and churches have no authority to administer civil laws.

The canon of Scripture was completed, about 90 to 95 A.D., when John wrote the Book of Revelation. God had completely revealed all that man needed to know about God, to be saved, and live for God. The word "canon" means "rule or measuring stick." Thus, the canon is the list of the inspired books of the Bible. God affirmed the inspiration of His word saying, "All scripture is given by inspiration of God, and is profitable for doctrine, for reproof, for correction, for instruction in righteousness: That the man of God may be perfect, throughly furnished unto all good works." (2 Timothy 3:16-17)

Another important principle to understand is that when God revealed a principle in the Old Testament, it was eternal and never was invalidated or changed by later revelation. God stated in Revelation 22:18-19, that no man should ever add to or subtract from the Scriptures. Take for example the Law given at Mt. Sinai. Today Christians do not live by the letter of the law, but the principles on which the laws were based are eternally valid. Even though Christians are not literally under the Law, the principles of the Law given at Mt. Sinai is still valid today.

"Concerning thy testimonies, I have known of old that thou hast founded them for ever." (Psalms 119:152)

"Thy word is true from the beginning: and every one of thy righteous judgments endureth for ever." (Psalms 119:160)

"For verily I say unto you, Till heaven and earth pass, one jot or one tittle shall in no wise pass from the law, till all be fulfilled." (Matthew 5:18)
"Heaven and earth shall pass away, but

my words shall not pass away." (Matthew 24:35)

"But the word of the Lord endureth for ever. And this is the word which by the gospel is preached unto you." (1 Peter 1:25)

It is important to understand the Bible's principles do not change in time because God does not change. God is immutable, meaning unchanging. The scriptures state "For I am the LORD, I change not; therefore ye sons of Jacob are not consumed." (Malachi 3:6) Other passages that teach this truth about God are Numbers 23:19; 1 Samuel 15:29; Isaiah 46:9-11; Ezekiel 24:14; James 1:17. Also:

"The counsel of the LORD standeth for ever, the thoughts of his heart to all generations." (Psalms 33:11)

"Blessed be the LORD God of Israel from everlasting, and to everlasting. Amen, and Amen." (Psalms 41:13)

"Before the mountains were brought forth, or ever thou hadst formed the earth and the world, even from everlasting to everlasting, thou art

> *God." (Psalms 90:2)*
>
> *"Thou turnest man to destruction; and sayest, Return, ye children of men." (Psalms 90:3)*
>
> *"For a thousand years in thy sight are but as yesterday when it is past, and as a watch in the night." (Psalms 90:4)*

This passage further explains that God's revelation to man was completed with the Book of Revelation and He has inspired no further scriptures. He has given man all He intended to reveal to us and it is sufficient. We do not need further revelation.

Customs, culture, political situations may change and this in turn may change the way the principle is applied. However, the principle itself does not change, nor the interpretation. The Law says we are to *"have no other God before thee."* (Deut. 5:7) That is as true now as it was then.

For an example, in Deut. 7:1f, God instructs Israel to be separated from the wicked peoples of Canaan. In 2 Corinthians 6:14, the same principle is being applied to the Christians being unequally yoked with unbelievers. The Bible says to Church Age believers, "Be ye not unequally yoked together with unbelievers: for what fellowship hath righteousness with unrighteousness? and what communion hath light with darkness? And what concord hath Christ with Belial? or what part hath he that believeth with an infidel?" (2 Corinthians 6:14-15) In both passages, God is teaching us the Doctrine of Separation. Time changed the people involved, the manner of separation, and a host of other details, yet, it is the same principle is applied in both the Old and New Testaments. The principle is clear that a passage of Scripture can only have one meaning or interpretation, but in different circumstances can have different applications.

When interpreting God's word, we must understand that God revealed His word over a long period of time, but what He revealed was absolutely consistent with what He had previously or later revealed. The interpretation of a passage to be accurate must consider when the scripture was penned and what God was revealing at that time.

Grant One Interpretation to Each Passage

When the words of Scripture were penned, they had only one meaning. We should search for that one meaning. To accept multiple interpretations for one scripture passage causes confusion and is inaccurate. Scripture itself does not allow for multiple interpretations of a verse. Note that we are talking about the interpretation of a passage and not about the application. A passage can have several applications, however in its historical, cultural, and grammatical setting; it can have only one interpretation or meaning.

God promised the Nation of Israel would inherit the area of land from river in Egypt (referring to the Nile) in the south, to the Euphrates River in the north. (Genesis 15:18) It is incorrect to interpret this verse in any other way, but to say God literally promised this land to Abraham's descendants. It does not mean God made these promises to churches or anyone else and it applies only to Israel. The Euphrates River does not mean the Persian Gulf or any other body of water, nor does it have a mystical meaning. It has only one meaning and that meaning must govern the interpretation of a verse or passage. In other words, Israel will inherit and live in that specific geographical land exactly as God promised them.

This rule of granting only one interpretation of a passage is violated often in the study of the parables. A parable is a simile and metaphor, which was used by Christ to illustrate a particular point or truth in a discourse. Jesus used sixty parables in His preaching to illustrate the principles he was teaching.

A good example of the improper interpretation of a parable is the allegorical interpretation of

Augustine (355-430 AD) of the parable of the Good Samaritan. Augustine said the man who was attacked stands for Adam; Jerusalem, the heavenly city from which he has fallen; the thieves, the devil who strips Adam of his immortality and leads him to sin; the priest and Levite, the Old Testament Law and ministry which was unable to cleanse and save anyone; the good Samaritan who binds the wounds. Christ who forgives sin; oil and wine; are hope and stimulus to work, the animal, the incarnation; the inn, the church; and the innkeeper, the apostle Paul.[23] The question one should ask is on what basis did Augustine come up with this elaborate interpretation? Plainly, that is not what the text states. Of course, the answer is he used his own imagination to allegorize the parable.

How then should this parable be interpreted? The answer is to let the Bible interpret itself! In the giving, the parable of the Good Samaritan recorded in Luke 10:30-37, Jesus was answering the question asked by a lawyer who sought to tempt Him. The lawyer asked what should he do to inherit eternal life? (Luke 10:25) Jesus asked the lawyer what was written in the Law meaning the Old Testament scriptures. The lawyer quoted Deuteronomy 6:5 and Leviticus 19:18. Jesus replied that the lawyer's answer was correct and for him to do this and live. However, the lawyer seeking to justify himself through good works asked who was his neighbor? The pious and proud Jews excluded Samaritans and Gentiles from being their neighbors. Jesus knew this and used the parable to expose the hypocrisy of the lawyer. In Luke, 10:36, after concluding the parable, Jesus asked the lawyer who he thought was the neighbor in the parable. The lawyer replied, *"he that showed mercy on him."* Jesus then told the lawyer *"Go and do likewise."* There is no hidden meaning in this illustration. It was given to present one meaning. The lawyer's answer showed he understood this and correctly responded to Jesus' question. To allegorize this parable or use it to teach anything else other than it was to answer the question "who is my neighbor" is a false interpretation and not meant by God.

In John 7:24-29, Jesus gave the parable of the two men who built houses. The wise man built his house on a rock and when the rain and floods came, it stood because it had a firm foundation. The wise man built his house on a rock and when the rain and floods came, it stood because it had a firm foundation.

However, the foolish man built on sand and when the rain and floods came it was destroyed because it had no foundation.

Considering the context of the parable the interpretation is plain. Jesus had just stated that

"Enter ye in at the strait gate: for wide is the gate, and broad is the way, that leadeth to destruction, and many there be which go in thereat: Because strait is the gate, and narrow is the way, which leadeth unto life, and few there be that find it." (Matthew 7:13-14)

Further, Jesus spoke of false prophets and explained that "Not every one that saith unto me, Lord, Lord, shall enter into the kingdom of heaven; but he that doeth the will of my Father which is in heaven. Many will say to me in that day, Lord, Lord, have we not prophesied in thy name? and in thy name have cast out devils? and in thy name done many wonderful works? And then will I profess unto them, I never knew you: depart from me, ye that work iniquity." (Matthew 7:21-23)

There is a single interpretation of the passage and the parable which Jesus revealed saying, "Therefore whosoever heareth these sayings of mine, and doeth them, I will liken him unto a wise man, which built his house upon a rock:" (Matthew 7:24) Some foolishly try to give a spiritual meaning to each aspect of the parable such as the rain, flood, wind, rocks, etc. There is no other meaning but literally what Jesus meant by the words He used.

Therefore, grant a parable only one interpretation. A parable is given to illustrate one point or truth and should not be to "walk on all fours."[24] The interpretation of a parable is the point of the narrative as a whole. The details of the illustration are not the topic of the parable and should not be pulled out of the narrative and expounded on.

Choose the Simplest Alternative

In a very few instances the correct interpretation is not clear. This is a rare occurrence. There is a classic example of this found in Judges 11:30-40. Jephthah, made a vow that if God would grant him victory in battle, whatever met him coming out of the doors of his house when he returned home, he would sacrifice in a burnt offering to the Lord. When He returned home, he was met by his daughter! Judges 11:39 states that he honored his vow. The popular interpretation is that she was literally sacrificed as a burnt offering. In fact, most of the early Jewish commentators and all the Christian Fathers for ten or eleven centuries, such as Origen, Chrysostom, Theodoret, Jerome, Augustine, etc. all held this view. But are we to let popular opinion or tradition dictate the interpretation or let the passage tell us?

Others take their interpretation from the passage itself and conclude that she was offered as a perpetual virgin to serve in the temple the rest of her life. Both sides of this debate have seemingly valid reasons to accept their view. However, does the passage give a clue as to what transpired?

Note that the Bible says the daughter went into the mountains for two months of mourning to "bewail her virginity" with her friends. Why would the Lord include this statement if she was to be offered as a burnt sacrifice? In addition, why did the women in Israel each year go for four days to the lament in honor her loyalty and personal sacrifice? It does not say they wanted to remember her life, but rather her virginity. How then is this passage to be interpreted? Her virginity would refer to her not being married and not having children.

First, considering the analogy of the faith, it must be considered that God would never condone or accept human sacrifice. This is totally out of character for God to allow her to be killed and sacrificed thus that result would not be valid.

The simpler explanation is that Jephthah gave her up to temple service to be a perpetual virgin. Judges 11:37 says his daughter went for two months into the mountains to "bewail her virginity." This statement is vital to understanding the interpretation of the event. The daughter was his only child, and because of honoring his vow, Jephthah would have no descendants. This was a serious matter in eastern culture. The tragedy was that Jephthah's lineage would end because of his imprudent vow.

His daughter also "bewailed her virginity"

because she as a faithful daughter wished to give her father descendants, but because of his vow she would never marry and have children. What sacrifice Jephthah gave or sacrificed to the Lord was not having grandchildren and future descendants. In this example, we can see that historically both views cannot be right. She either lived or died, and one or the other is true, but not both. Judges 11:39, says the vow was kept and *"And it came to pass at the end of two months, that she returned unto her father, who did with her according to his vow which he had vowed: and she knew no man. And it was a custom in Israel."* The passage specifically states she remained a virgin. Some would purport that this is a "gray" area of scripture when the meaning is unclear. However, a careful study of the passage shows otherwise. In other words, she never married and was a virgin the rest of her life. To conclude she was given as a burnt off, is not acceptable from the wording of the text, or understanding that God would never condone human sacrifice for any reason.

We can honestly only allow one interpretation, because it can have only one. The simplest alternative is that she lived. This interpretation fits the culture of the time and does not violate the analogy of the faith. Thus, the proper understanding is she was not killed and sacrificed, but rather sacrificially never married. Consider that father would have to give his consent for her to be married and because of his vow he could not. She could not have been married and give her father grandchildren and his lineage ended. This interpretation violates none of the principles of interpreting God's word and clearly is what happened.

Never Invent Explanations to Silent Areas of Scripture

Simply stated, it means do not make up explanations to areas of Scripture that are silent and where God has not given us all the information about some topics of Scripture. For example, the Bible does not say where Heaven is. The Bible only indicates its direction is up. It is foolhardy to speculate that it is in some specific area of outer space. Some unwisely state they believe Heaven is in the northern area of space where astronomers report there are few stars. God did not tell us where heaven is, so we should not speculate and add to God's word.

Since this speculation was offered, the Hubble telescope has shown there are millions of stars in this region of space. Clearly, speculation serves no valid purpose because it is not based on any verifiable evidence. If the Bible is silent, we then too are to be silent. To offer one's personal speculation on some subject where the Bible is silent is actually adding to scripture. Many times, one person's stated speculation becomes another's belief. Another example is that Jesus said in Matthew 24:26 that only the Father knew when He would return, however, I once heard a well-known fundamentalist evangelist of national acclaim state at a Bible conference that when the planets aligned in 1984, the Rapture would occur. Many tracts were printed stating this view. Obviously, he was wrong. In the eyes of many people his testimony and credibility as a preacher was hurt. His predictions served no purpose. Another radio evangelist predicted and spent millions of dollars proclaiming Jesus would return on December 28, 2012. To his credit, he later apologized and admitted his obvious error.

It seems these end times prophets did not really believe Jesus' own words as He stated in Matthew 24:36. Further, they ignored the fact their predictions meant they knew more than God does and they are at liberty to contradict Him. Another negative result of such speculation is that these men profess they have special insight or spiritual abilities others do not have. Often these "prophets" print books and literature and made a great deal of money, which makes them suspect as a man of God. God stated in Deuteronomy 18:20 that if a prophet made a prophecy and it did not come true, he was to be put to death. It is a serious matter to tamper with God's word.

Literally, through the centuries, hundreds of dates have been proposed and every one of them has been wrong. It is adding to God's word to try to offer an explanation for silent areas of God's word. The rule is that if God is silent.... we should be silent.

Never Theorize to Accommodate Man's Views of Religion or Modern Science

This principle is closely aligned with the ninth principle. In interpreting Scripture, we should never invent explanations to areas where the Bible is vague. We may not have the knowledge necessary to understand some teaching or event in the Bible. The limitation is in our knowledge, not in the truth of the Word of God. When a man begins to speculate, he is in fact, trying to second-guess God! Such speculation casts a shadow over the credibility of the Bible and our faith. It does not convince the doubters and only brings confusion. The best approach is not to invent explanations, but honestly say we do not know!

The Gap Theory Speculation

Examples of man trying to harmonize science and the Bible are seen in theories such as "Theistic Evolution" and once popular but now debunked, "Gap Theory." Theistic evolution originated with man trying to fit the Bible into the false teachings of the so-called "science of evolution." In putting science before God's truth, some who profess they are Christians, have proposed what is called Theistic Evolution. They suppose that God used evolution and millions of years to create the world over a long period of time and they deny the literal meaning of Genesis Chapter One and Two. In truth, evolution contradicts the biblical account of Creation and denies God is our Creator. It calls God a liar calling the Genesis account of Creation a myth or at best an allegory. There is no possible way to make the two coincide being diametrically opposed to each other. Further, there is not one demonstrative evidence of evolution in true science. False science seeking to discredit the Bible and deny the existence of our God, or Creator proposed the hypothesis of "evolution." Evolution has no demonstrable evidence and thus is not a theory and only a hypothesis or unsubstantiated guess with no evidence to support it. Evolution purports the universe and life came into existence by random chance and there is no Designer and no God. Man, then, is the product of some unobservable and unrepeatable process whereby life was randomly and accidentally generated from inert matter. True science proves life does not come from inert matter. Inert means to have no power to act, or react with other minerals. In putting false science before God's truth, the theistic evolutionist supposes that God used evolution to create the world over long periods of time and they deny the literal meaning of Genesis Chapter One and Two. One must understand that God's Word is perfect and without error. It is inerrant, and infallible.

When God said, He created the universe and the earth in six days, by speaking it into existence out of nothing, (exhilo) then that is the Word of God on the matter and the truth. In Exodus, God plainly stated "For in six days the LORD made heaven and earth, the sea, and all that in them is, and rested the seventh day: wherefore the LORD blessed the Sabbath day, and hallowed it." (Exodus 20:11) A six-day creation precluded there being a prior creation. If science disagrees with the Bible, then science is wrong! Science is the product of man's fallible wisdom, which is proven faulty and always changing. The Bible is the very Word of God who is never wrong and do not change! Their false assumption denies God's word and calls Him a liar, and not omniscient meaning know all things without exception.

True science is based on provable, demonstrable, empirical evidence. God created the Universe, its physical laws and science, and it cannot contradict Him. Evolution cannot be proven or demonstrated, because it is a myth. True science is truth.

The principle is that the only way to know the truth is to examine it using the "looking glass" of the Bible. In other words, we are to take the Bible and examine everything by it, including the theories of science. It is the ONLY true standard. It is the only pure source of truth on earth.

If the Bible says there was a worldwide flood the true believer accepts this as absolute truth. He finds the physical evidence that is seen all over the world which scientifically substantiates what the Bible states. The world's way is the opposite. A man with a sinful and darkened mind examines the Bible, refuses to believe it, and declares it invalid in spite of the refutable he sees. Man starts out with a distorted view and can only come to a distorted and false conclusion. God explains this saying, "But the natural man receiveth not the things of the Spirit of God: for they are foolishness unto him: neither can he know them, because they are spiritually discerned." (1 Corinthians 2:14)

Such theories, such as the Gap Theory, in no way have any value within themselves. This "theory" states that between Genesis 1:1 and 1:2, there is a gap in time in which the fossil record is placed. Its explanation is that the fossils are the remains of another race of man and a world that was destroyed when Lucifer rebelled in heaven, before the present world was created. This theory is based on man's speculations over one hundred years ago when evolution became popular. Men such as C. I. Scofield, under pressure by atheistic modern science, tried to accommodate the popular teachings of the then new "science" of evolution. Instead of accepting God's word, he and others theorized a gap in the Biblical record between Genesis 1:1 and 1:2. Dr. Scofield had a limited understanding of geology and few men in his day understood where the fossils came from. They could not explain the fossils and dinosaurs so they ignored what the Bible literally states and surmised there existed in a pre-historic world before the Genesis account of Creation. Today, we can easily explain the fossil record as being created by the Flood when God destroyed all life on earth, saving only Noah and his family and the animals in the ark. The fossils are the remains of the pre-flood world, preserved in the sedimentary rocks left by the Flood. It is not the remains of some world created and destroyed by God before the current Earth. True science proves that all fossils are found in sedimentary rock deposits. Sedimentary rock is formed by water action and is laid down in layers caused by a worldwide flood. Two things have perpetrated the false gap theory.

First, ignorance of the facts and second, a blatant disregard of the biblical principles of interpretation.

Today, evolution is falling into disfavor by honest scientists and even secular science is questioning the teaching of Darwin. Yet, today the Gap Theory is still being taught by a few proponents as fact, and yet it was never anything more than a man's theory or speculation. When I was in college, I asked one well known theology professor privately about the Gap Theory. He replied that he was a "smiling gapist." It seems he knew the truth, but for undisclosed reasons still taught it. Today, few biblical theologians hold or teach the view, but it will probably be many years before it completely disappears. A proper interpretation of scripture refutes this false teaching.

Trying to harmonize the teachings of evolution with the Bible, theologians in fact, have denied the Word of God. Let me at this point again reiterate that any false interpretation is personally attacking the Lord Jesus Himself. He is the Word and that means what He actually recorded for us. It is a gross sin when anyone does not diligently and accurately handle the Word of God. This brings to mind a mission's board director, who very pointedly told me God has given us great latitude with His Word. He used this statement to defend a clear violation of God's word.

God said He spoke the Universe into

existence "ex nihilo," meaning out of nothing. (Gen. 1) God says "In the beginning" meaning that before time existed there was nothing. Thus, God created time and the universe and the earth had a beginning. Evolution purports there was no beginning. God's word, then states, the universe did not evolve over millions of years or long periods of time as evolution postulates. The gap theory, in reality, instead of clarifying the matter of Creation caused confusion. It actually supports the false theory (lie) of evolution and Satan is the father of lies. (See John 8:44) Theistic evolution and the gap theory have aided in causing Christians to believe in the lie of evolution or some form of it denies God Himself. It caused many to doubt the Bible as God's infallible word. These false teachers added to God's word and aided Satan in opposing God.

Extra Biblical Teachings Contradict Scripture

Often beliefs and practices clearly contradict the Bible. Roman Catholics worship and pray to Mary. They say that she is the "mother of God" and teach she was a perpetual virgin, thus deifying Mary. Never in God's word is Mary, called the mother of God. She is called the "mother of Jesus" in John 2:1, 3, 19:25-26; and Acts 1:14. The Roman Catholic Church's faulty reasoning speculates that if Mary was Jesus' mother, and Jesus was God, then she was the mother of God! John 17:5 absolutely refutes this false speculation recording that Jesus said, "And now, O Father, glorify thou me with thine own self with the glory which I had with thee before the world was." Yes, Jesus Christ is God, incarnate in flesh and He is our eternal God, the Alpha and Omega. (Rev. 1:8, 11; 21:6; 22:13) Jesus said He was with the Father "before the world was." Mary, was simply the godly young woman who was chosen by God to be Jesus' physical mother and give Him His physical body. She could not be the mother of God because she did not give birth to God who is not a physical Being, but Spirit (John 4:24). God is eternally infinite and was not created. Jesus Christ is also infinite and as God was not created when He was born as a man. Mary was a physical person and therefore could not give birth to a spiritual being. Yes, Jesus is God incarnate in the flesh in that sense Mary gave birth to Jesus who is God. However, is a gross and a flagrant error to say Mary gave birth to God and therefore deify her, pray to her, and worship her. Further, never in God's word does God say we are to pray to anyone but God the Father, through Jesus Christ. (Matt. 6:9, Heb. 4:16)

In addition, the Bible states Mary and Joseph had four other sons, Joseph, James, Jude, and

Simon. (See Matt. 12:46; 13:55; Mark 6:3; John 2:12; 7:3, 5, 10; Acts 1:14; 1 Cor. 9:5; Gal. 1:19) This refutes the Roman Church teaching that Mary remained a perpetual virgin. Therefore, what the Roman Catholic Church believes and teaches is false doctrine that contradicts what the Bible teaches. This proves the Roman Church is a false church. It is a church that teaches lies, denies God's word, and thus serves Satan. This is but one of many false teachings of the Roman Church, which includes calling the Pope the vicar of Christ. (See Matt. 24:5, 11, 24)

The rule of correctly interpreting God's word is to let the Bible interpret itself. We should never invent teachings that are not clearly presented in scripture. Further, when the Bible is silent, we should be silent.

Never Base a Doctrine on One Passage of Scripture

No doctrine should be built on only one passage or verse of Scripture. Any true doctrine of God will be found in many places in the Bible. As mentioned earlier, the Mormons base their doctrine of baptisms for the dead on their misinterpretation of only one verse in the Bible. "Else what shall they do which are baptized for the dead, if the dead rise not at all? why are they then baptized for the dead?" (1 Corinthians 15:29).

(See page 50) Nowhere else in the Bible is the practice, even mentioned and this was never practiced by Christians. If you cannot find other places in the Bible that teaches the doctrine this should alert you to a problem. If the supposed doctrine is only found in one place, you should seek to find out why. In every case, you will discover that what is being taught is not a doctrine. To arrive at the correct understanding of a teaching (doctrine) in Scripture you must study all related texts and then put them together. Until you do this, it is difficult to know that you have all the truth revealed on a particular subject. It would be wrong to formulate a doctrine from the statements in a parable.

An example of basing a doctrine or practice on one passage of scripture is done when 1 Corinthians 14:14-15 is misinterpreted. Plainly, the New Testament does not teach that "tongues" was a prayer language and the only time prayer is mentioned with tongues it is condemned. (1 Cor. 14:14) Paul, in 1 Corinthians 14 is refuting the unscriptural practice of glossolalia. Ecstatic speech was not biblical speaking of an unlearned language. Note that in Acts 2:4, Luke uses the phrase "other tongues" (heteros glossia = other language). In 1 Corinthians 14 Paul uses the word same word "glossa" (tongue).

The word in our English Bibles "unknown" was

added by the King James Bible translators, but it is not found in any Koine Greek text. Instead of "unknown" a better word would have been "unlearned." The text should *read* "For he that speaketh in an ~~unknown~~ tongue (language) speaketh not unto men, but unto God: for no man understandeth him; howbeit in the spirit he speaketh mysteries." Paul then proceeds to condemn in strong language what the Corinthians were doing. He states those practicing this unscriptural utterance is not to man and that no man understands what is being said. The key is found in 1 Corinthians 14:4, "He that speaketh in an ~~unknown~~ tongue edifieth himself; but he that prophesieth edifieth the church." In other words, the false tongues speaker does not benefit anyone but himself in that he receives an emotional high from his activity. When uttering *glossa* a person appears to be directed by the Holy Spirit, which makes him look spiritual to those who hear him. Further, it makes the "modern tongues speaker" feel emotional and is deceived into thinking he has a special gift from God. Paul states plainly that that was not the purpose of biblical tongues, "For he that speaketh in an unknown tongue speaketh not unto men, but unto God: for no man understandeth him; howbeit in the spirit he speaketh mysteries." 1 Corinthians 14:13 says, "Wherefore let him that speaketh in an *unknown* tongue pray that he may interpret." In other words, let the person who is practicing *glossa* pray that he may be an interpreter of God's word.

1 Corinthians 14:22 clearly refutes that biblical tongues are given as a special prayer language or for the emotional benefit of a believer. It says, "Wherefore tongues are for a sign, **not to them that believe, but to them that believe not**: but prophesying *serveth* not for them that believe not, but for them which believe. (1 Corinthians 14:22) Biblical tongues as spoken in the early churches was a tool of evangelism to authenticate the Gospel as coming from God and that the apostles were men of God. These verses clearly refute the use of tongues as being given to benefit the tongues speaker. Biblical tongues are not valid today as 1 Corinthians 13:8 explains. "Charity never faileth: but whether *there be* prophecies, they shall fail; whether *there be* tongues, they shall cease; whether *there be* knowledge, it shall vanish away." (1 Corinthians 13:8)

CHAPTER SEVEN
Concluding Statement

In trying to determine what the Scriptures mean we must have a method or standard of interpretation as a guide. The literal or the Historical, Cultural, and Grammatical method stands alone as the only real biblical method. Applying God's principles of interpretation are simple. We should accept God's word as what it literally states. Why? Because they are the words of God given by inspiration and the best interpreter is God Himself, and by letting Scripture interpret Scripture, we are letting God, the Author of the Bible tells us what He means by what He said.

As a person begins to apply these principles or rules of interpretation, he will become more proficient and skilled. We all should be students of the Bible, and hone our skills in the Word of God that we might be better instruments to reach others for Christ. God has commanded each of us to be Bible students and teachers. (2 Tim. 2:15) Our responsibility is to **KNOW** the Word ourselves that we might be able to feed our own spiritual souls by feasting on the sincere meat of God's Word. Correctly knowing God's word, then, enables us to help others and teach them so they too can grow.

The love of God is the best motivation for the

believer to follow Christ. This love comes from knowing God. We can only know Him from His Word, which is the Bible. This is the power of correctly interpreting the Bible. This method teaches the pure Word of God as the Holy Spirit guides, inspires and nourishes us as we study. All Christians are teachers. We teach at home, work and in the daily routines of life. Some Christians have the privilege to teach from pulpits, some in classes such as Sunday School and in Bible Study Classes. No matter what your background, teaching this method will be of help to you.

For those without formal college training this course can teach them how to study the Bible. It will help the pastor whose training has been limited to become competent in understanding God's word. The Sunday School teacher after applying these principles will be better able to teach from the Bible and be less dependent on some else's prepared lessons. It will teach the believer to feed himself from God's Word and become confident in their knowledge of the Bible. Applying this principle will enable the student of the scriptures to "Preach the word; be instant in season, out of season; reprove, rebuke, exhort with all longsuffering and doctrine." (2 Timothy 4:2)

DEFINITIONS:

Allegory. Taking the literal meaning of the

story, discourse, or something written and giving it another spiritualized or non- literal meaning.

Analogy. Similarity between things partial resemblance. Comparing something point by point with something else noting its similarity. As applied to Bible study, it means the scriptures are alike and do not contradict each other.

Context. The parts of a book, passage or verse, which shows the whole situation and relevant environment in which it is found.

Expository. Setting forth facts, ideas, and an explanation from a detailed examination of a passage.

Exegesis. Critical analysis or interpretation which seeks the meaning from the passage and does not impose meaning on the passage.

Interpretation. To arrive at the original meaning the writer intended when he penned the words.

Syntax. Syntax is the study of the word in is grammatical setting showing its relation to other words.

APPENDIX

A LIST OF STUDY HELPS AND REFERENCE BOOKS

BIBLE HANDBOOKS

Halley's Bible Handbook, Henry H. Halley, Zondervan Publishing House

Unger's Bible Handbook, Merrill F. Unger, Moody Press

A Bible Handbook is arranged by the Books and Chapters of the Bible. It contains a wealth of information about the Bible. It includes, as the title page of Halley's Bible Handbook states, "A General View of the Bible, Heart thoughts of the Bible, Remarkable Archaeological Discoveries, Notes on Each of The Bible Books, Miscellaneous Bible Information, Notes on Obscure Passages, Related Historical Data, An Epitome of Church History, Suggestion on Church-Going." This information is invaluable in understanding the historical situation of the Scripture you are investigating.

There are many pictures, charts and diagrams found throughout the handbook that greatly aids in understanding the historical situation of portions of Scripture. For example, the reference to Genesis

10-11, gives a great deal of information concerning Egyptian history, including the Egyptian dynasties, past wars, and chronology of the period. This background information will help you to understand the period of time between the Flood and Abraham.

BIBLE DICTIONARIES

Unger's Bible Dictionary, Merrill F. Unger, Moody Press, Chicago.

Zondervan's Pictorial Dictionary of the Bible, Merrill C. Tenney, Zondervan Publishing House, Grand Rapids, Mich.

Nelson's Illustrated Bible Dictionary, Herbert Lockyer, Thomas Nelson Publishers, Nashville, Camden, New York.

Holman Illustrated Bible Dictionary, Chad Brand, Archie England and Charles W. Draper.

A Bible Dictionary is an alphabetical listing of the all the major words found in the Bible with their meanings. A Bible Dictionary is more like an encyclopedia than just a simple word dictionary. For example: it will list all the proper names found in the Bible, with not only its pronunciation and meaning, but also will give information about the various persons in the Bible that had that name with related Scripture references. A Bible Dictionary will furnish information on such things as money, tools, customs, geography, cities, towns and countries. It will list each Book of the Bible with an outline and historical data, such as the author, date, addressee, subject and content.

A CONCORDANCE OF THE BIBLE

Strong's Exhaustive Concordance of the Bible, James Strong, MacDonald Publishing Company.

Young's Analytical Concordance of the Bible, Robert Young, Wm. B. Eerdmans Publishing Company.

Layman's English-Greek Concordance, James Gall, Baker Book House, Grand Rapids, Michigan, 1975

The Englishman's Greek Concordance of the New Testament, George V. Wigram, Baker Book House, Grand Rapids, Mich., 1979.

A Bible concordance is an alphabetical listing of every word found in the Bible with every verse in which it is used listed. If you know only one word of a verse, you can use a concordance to find the reference you are looking for. The first two concordances listed above are "exhaustive concordances." This means that every occurrence of the word in the Bible is listed. Condensed concordances have only limited use, as they do not list every occurrence of a word in Scripture. Strong's is probably the most popular concordance. In addition to being a concordance, it includes a Hebrew and Greek dictionary of Bible words.

Strong has assigned each Hebrew and Greek word in the Bible with a number. This numbering system is used by most other reference books, making Strong's Concordance a must for Bible students.

The Layman's English-Greek Concordance lists all the English words of the Bible. However, under each English word is listed the various Greek words from which it was translated with references. For example: If you were to look up the English word "accompany" you would find that no less than five Greek words are translated "accompany" in our English Bible. Each of the five Greek words has a slightly different meaning. By looking up the definition of the Greek word in a word study book such as Vines Complete Expository Dictionary of Old and New Testament words, you would have a better understanding of the passage of Scripture.

The Englishman's Greek Concordance of the New Testament, is a Greek concordance, (written in English), arranged using the Strong's Concordance word numbering system. Without being able to read Greek, a word can be located in

English in <u>Strong's Concordance</u> and then using Strong's numbers can be used to find the exact Greek word in <u>The Englishman's Greek Concordance</u>. The Greek words are arranged alphabetically and each verse the Greek word is used in the New Testament is shown. This is invaluable in determining the exact Greek word used and its proper meaning.

WORD STUDY BOOKS

<u>Vine's Complete Expository Dictionary of Old and New Testament Words</u>, W. E. Vine, Merrill F. Unger, William White, Jr., Thomas Nelson Publishers. Nashville, 1984

<u>Theological Word Book of the Old Testament</u>, Harris, Archer, Waltke, Moody Press, Chicago.

<u>Word Study Greek-English New Testament: with complete concordance</u>, Paul R. McReynolds, Tyndale.

<u>Word Pictures in the New Testament</u>, A. T. Robertson, Baker.

Word study books list the words used in the Bible with their Greek or Hebrew meaning. (Hebrew for the Old Testament and Greek for the New Testament) These study helps are invaluable in determining the original meaning of the words of the Bible. Our English words were translated from Hebrew or Greek and often one English word was used to translate several words in the original language. It is important to know which Hebrew or Greek word the English word represents in order to determine its correct definition.

COMMENTARIES

The Wycliffe Bible Commentary, Charles F. Pfeiffer, Everette Harrison, Moody Press, Chicago.

Matthew Henry's Commentary on the Bible, Matthew Henry, MacDonald Publishing Company, McLean, VA.

Romans, Donald Grey Barnhouse, Wm. B. Eerdmans Publishing Company, Grand Rapids, Mich.

The Bible Knowledge Commentary, An Exposition of the Scriptures by Dallas Seminary Faculty, Old and New Testament, John F. Walvoord, Roy B. Zuck, Victor Books, 1988. (Caution: Based on the New International Version of the Bible)

A Commentary on the Holy Bible, Matthew Poole, Hendrickson.

A Commentary on the Old and New Testament, Jamieson, Fausset, and Brown, Hendrickson.

Thru the Bible. J. Vernon McGee, Nelson (Use with caution)

A commentary is the written comments and explanatory notes of an author on Scripture. Many commentaries are available covering the entire

Bible or just one Book. When consulting commentaries be sure to investigate the author. This information will be found on cover sheets of most books. Where the author went to school, the denomination he belongs to, what Bible version he uses, and other information will guide you in determining his position on the Scriptures. <u>Just because a person writes a commentary on Scripture is no assurance what he writes will be doctrinally sound.</u>

Commentaries can greatly aid in studying the Bible, but be aware they can become a crutch if we are not careful. Use them to get different perspectives on a passage of Scripture. Be aware commentators can make errors in judgment and come to incorrect conclusions. The rule is to use them as a guide, but never as an authority. The Bible itself is our only authority. It is the Bible that judges whether the commentator is correct.

The three commentaries above are very popular and are representative of most commentaries. They would be a good addition to your library. The first two are commentaries on the whole Bible and are good "general" reference to the Scriptures. Verse by verse commentaries focus on a smaller portion of Scripture and will give more detailed information than would be possible in a commentary covering the entire Bible. Purchasing several commentaries on one book will help you get a better and wider perspective on the book you are studying.

STUDY BIBLES

The Ryrie Study Bible, Charles Caldwell Ryrie, Moody Press, Chicago.

The Scofield Reference Bible, C. I. Scofield, Oxford University Press, New York.

The Thompson Chain Reference Bible, Frank Charles Thompson, B. B. Kirkbride Bible Co., Inc.

A Study Bible is one in which an author has written explanatory notes in the margins, but also use caution. Study Bibles will have much information that aids in understanding the Bible. Modern words are given for antiquated ones. Cross-references are included to guide the reader to other places in Scripture where the subject of the verse is found in parallel passages or other places in scripture. Some contain abbreviated Bible dictionaries and concordances that can be very useful.

ABOUT THE AUTHOR

 Dr. Cooper Abrams is a veteran missionary, pastor, church planter, and author working in the state of Utah since 1986. He and his wife Carolyn are missionaries sent by Calvary Baptist Church, King, NC and have been involved in seeing three sound Independent Baptist churches established in Utah since 1986 and assisting other churches in Utah, Wyoming, and Idaho.

He graduated from Piedmont Baptist College in 1981 with a Th.B. (Bachelor of Theology), and in 2000 with an MBS (Master of Biblical Studies). In 2013, he earned a PhD in Religion - Bible Major from Bethany Divinity College and Seminary.

He is an avid writer and has authored numerous articles, books, Bible courses, and six Bible commentaries. His has written many articles on apologetics, hermeneutics, Baptist History, The Pentecostal Movement, and Mormonism.

Most of his work is posted on his popular Internet web site, Bible Truth http://bible-truth.org. The web site which was begun in 1996 currently averages thousands each month. The site is rated as one of the top two to five Baptist web sites, out of thousands on the Internet.

He can be contacted at:
435 452-1716
http://bible-truth.org
cpabrams3@gmail.com

Calvary Baptist Church
P.O. Box 536
King, NC 27021

End Notes

[1] Paul Lee Tan, Literal Interpretation of the Bible (Rockville, Maryland: Assurance Publishers, 1978) p. 9.

[2] Hermeneutics is the science of interpretation, especially of Scripture. It is a branch of theology that deals with principles and methodology of exegesis.

[3] An allegory is an extended metaphor. Biblical example: "Which things are an allegory: for these are the two covenants; the one from the Mount Sinai, which gendereth to bondage, which is Agar. (Galatians 4:24)

[4] John Bunyan, *The Pilgrim's Progress from This World to That Which Is to Come*, Grand Rapids: Thomas Nelson,1678)

[5] Tan, p.25.

[6] "De Principiis IV, 16" (http://www.ewtn.com/library/PATRISTC/ANF4-14.HTM#Bk IV)

[7] Reformed and Replacement theology teach that God is finished with Israel and that the "church" has replaced Israel and will receive God's promises made to them.

[8] W.E. Vines, An Expository Dictionary of New Testament Words, (Nashville: Thomas Nelson, 1985) p. 102.

[9] Dictionary.com (http://dictionary.reference.com/browse/church?s=t)

[10] Colin Brown, The New International Dictionary of New Testament Theology. 3 vols. (Grand Rapids: Zondervan, 1979), p. 291.

[11] "Catholic" means universal in extent, thus a worldwide church.

[12] Dispensationalism. A system of order, government, or organization of a nation, community, etc., especially as existing at a particular time. (in Christian theology) a divinely ordained order prevailing at a particular period of history.

[13] Charles Caldwell Ryrie, Dispensationalism Today (Chicago: Moody Press) 1965.

[14] Salvation in all ages has always been by God's grace, so to describe today as the Age of Grace is not completely accurate. The term must be understood as referring to the freedom from the Mosaic Law that believers have in this dispensation of the institution of the local church. The term is used to differentiate between law and grace.

[15] Robertson, p.

[16] The **tallit** katan (also pronounced *tallis*) is a prayer shawl, the most authentic **Jewish** garment. It is a rectangular-shaped piece of linen or wool (and sometimes, now, polyester or silk) with special fringes called "tzitzit" on each of the four corners. The purpose of the garment is to hold the Tzitzit.
(http://www.templesanjose.org/JudaismInfo/faq/tallit.htm)

[17] A "theophany" is an appearance of God.

[18] A "Christophany" is a pre-incarnate appearance of Jesus Christ.

[19] Paul Lee Tan, The Interpretation of Prophecy

ENDNOTES

(Rockville, MD: Assurance Publishers, 1974) p.106.

Vines, p.140.

Robertson, p. 518.

Vines, p.420.

[23]

http://www.bible.org/page.php?page_id=2114#P12_1242.

Tan, p.74

9 781732 174689